Poems and Stories About Life

Keith Sheets

"Thy word is a lamp unto my feet, and a light unto my path"
Psalm 119:105

Poems and Stories About Life

Keith Sheets

CITI OF
BOOKS

CITIOFBOOKS, INC.
3736 Eubank NE Suite A1
Albuquerque, NM 87111-3579
www.citiofbooks.com
Hotline: 1 (877) 389-2759
Fax: 1 (505) 930-7244

Ordering Information:
Quantity sales. Special discounts are available on quantity purchases by corporations, associations, and others. For details, contact the publisher at the address above.

Printed in the United States of America.

ISBN-13:	Softcover	979-8-89391-282-1
	eBook	979-8-89391-283-8

Library of Congress Control Number: 2024917379

Table of Contents

POEMS

The Farm

To be reared on the farm is like receiving A special favor of God

To be so close to the wonderful world of nature

To see new life every spring

Baby calves, baby pigs, tender buds greening

A seed of corn pushing up for life

The smell of fresh plowed earth

The sight of many gulls feeding behind the plow

Yes, to be reared on the farm is

A very special treat

KS 1972

Stars

To lie at night and look into the sky

Is to explore the unknown to the fullest extent

To wonder what each little light represent

Whether it is a ball of fire or another planet of life

Oh, what a thrill to imagine another planet with life

To see a shooting star is an awesome sight.

The streak of fire across the sky

And then to know that the light is gone forever.

Yes, there is no greater experience than to

 Look into the sky at night.

KS 1973

To The Agriculturist

Be a good keeper of the soil.

Your job is so very important.

Feeding the world by tilling the soil.

The productivity of the earth Depends on you

Keep the soil healthy

Free from erosion and misuse

Yes, we beg of you

Be a good keeper of the soil

KS 1973

The Mind

Is the mind like a jungle of electrical connections?
Is it like ribbons of unknown probing into space?
Man has attained great knowledge in
A vast area of subjects.
His abilities seem to be unlimited.
He knows how to split atoms
And how molecules are formed
But why doesn't he know—
His own mind?

KS 1973

How Far Should Man Fly

God made birds to fly.

God did not give man wings

Did God make man to fly?

If God made man to fly,

How far is he to soar in his powerful rockets?

Just to the moon or far beyond?

What would God say

If man flew into his kingdom and said,

"Look God, I can fly"

God would likely say,

"This makes me happy man

For I gave you a very special brain

And a quest for knowledge

So fly man.

Fly, as far as you can."

KS 1973

Progress

Man has made tremendous progress with his machines

A vast area of problems has been solved with technology

Factories are humming

Progress is evident

But hark, the machines and factories are using

And polluting the very air we breathe

And the water we drink. Now, is the time for caution.

To stop and think

About machines, technology, and the harm that could come.

We must be careful and not forget

And become so engrossed in our progress

That we eliminate—ourselves?

KS 1973

Election Year

Every four years Americans are wooed, you see,
By the crafty politicians
Of this great country.
Promises are made, issues are discussed,
And the picture is painted that
Generally, the country is in a sorry state
And things will get much better
If we will only elect a certain candidate.
When the election is over and the
Smoke is cleared
Americans have another four years of
What could have been feared

Loneliness

Loneliness is a stranger to no person

It may come and linger a while inside you

It may come when a close relative passes on

It may come when a spouse forgets or neglects

But how will you know when loneliness comes?

You will know—

By the feeling deep down inside you

By the dull ache that stays inside you until loneliness leaves

Yes, you will know my friend,

When loneliness visits you.

KS 1973

Death

Death does not discriminate
It calls on the rich as well as the poor
It calls on the young as well as the old
It calls on the Christian as well as the heathen
It may come with or without warning
A passing thought might be
"How could I have lived my life different?"
"What could I have done to make it count?"
It matters not
For in the hand of fate
Death, truly, does not discriminate

KS 1973

Wife

To my darling wife

Whose love I am so fortunate to receive

For she does her very best

To make all of us believe

That she is the best mother and wife

That anyone ever had

In their whole entire life

And it is true by golly we say

If you don't believe us,

Just follow her around

For one single day

November 10, 1973

Sleeping Between Two Big Brothers

I had my choice

I could either sleep in the middle

And be squeezed and smothered

Or sleep on the outside

And be half uncovered

Of course, in that house, I chose the squeeze

Because before morning, it would surely freeze

We really slept warm, don't you see?

Without electric blankets or other energy.

Things could have been worse, by living in Alaska

But we lived on a dry land farm in Nebraska

And sometimes, I long for the return of those good old days

When families were closer in many ways

But we know they will never return

So we look to the future with some concern

KS 1975

Horse Manure

The smell was for sure

It was pure horse manure

But my brothers said it had to dry many hours in the sun

To burn in the corn cob pipe they made with fun

It burned hotter than some tobacco they say

But in those days, there was no money to pay

Things were going very fine you see

Until their pipe burned my bare belly

Being less than five years of age

I went bawling to Mom with tears of rage

And when Mom asked what they were smoking and what was stinking

I blurted out the answer without even thinking

I hope my brothers have forgiven me for that day

When I told Mom and spoiled their play

KS 1975

Official Ambassador

Be it known that from the Ukpaka household
That Carolyn is the one that should be told,
That she is to be the Ambassador to Nigeria from Nebraskaland
To spread good will and tell it firsthand.
The people will want to know about the land from which she came,
For they will know that for her and her husband, it couldn't be the same.
She has lived in Nebraska for many a year,
And experienced all kinds of weather without any fear.
Tornados, hail, sleet, rain, snow, we have it all;
If it doesn't come in the spring, it will in the fall.
And occasionally, we have a wind right out of the south.
That will blow a spoken word right back into the mouth.
Now, the people of Nigeria may think there is no hell;
But if they have never experienced a Nebraska blizzard, how can they tell?
And don't forget to tell what it's like on "Big Red" day
When seventy thousand nuts come to town awhile and stay.
And tell them about your husband, that remarkable little man;
He came to Nebraska and accomplished more than most people can.
He worked real hard and earned a master's degree;
And Lord only knows, it sure wasn't free.
He worked in Water Quality along with Sue Hoppel;
And even while waiting for the red dye, he did not topple.
Tell them how he received a promotion from Nigeria one day,
And from then on there was really nothing that could make him stay.
They even made him an Admiral in the Nebraska Navy,
But that still wasn't nearly enough gravy.
So, we hope the two of you don't forget Nebraska and this day,
And don't forget us unlucky ones that really have to stay.
So, go tell them Carolynn. Tell it like it is.
And from all of us to both of you, "best of luck, Gee Whiz

(Written for a co-worker's farewell party KS 1975)

Miracles

The little country hospital halls
Were empty and lonely at early morning.
Many miles had been walked
In those halls that night.
And outside a spring blizzard was
raging as winter made its last appearance.
And then, I heard a sound;
 I had been waiting for.
It sent a chilling feeling, a feeling of
awe throughout my body—
from my face to the very
tips of my toes.
I realized that God's wonderful
miracles were still happening when
I heard that sound.
Of course, the sound was the
cry of a newborn baby.
You see, my first son had
just taken his first breath.

KS 1975

To Mom and Dad

I have never written you any kind of poem

To tell you how I really appreciated you at home

To tell you that, at times, I have felt quite sad

For the disrespect that I showed when I was a teen lad

But so it seems the nature of man from the start

He has to be so old to be just a little smart

But I have come to realize during the recent years

That you folks really deserve a lot of cheers

For raising us the special way you did

For good guidance is important for any kid

You always emphasized honesty to a high degree

And that has had a very special meaning for me

So, I am writing this poem for this year's Mother's and Father's day

To show a deep appreciation that I never before would say

And just let me add before I am through

That I am very proud to have parents like you

Love,

Keith

KS 1977

NRC's Loss Is Butler County's Gain

In 1977, they sent a Federal man

To help the State people with the 208 Plan.

He participated in workshops throughout the State

He attended many meetings and was very seldom late.

Whenever a dispute or a controversial issue would arise

He handled it with diplomacy, which was really no surprise.

He tackled his work with a great deal of enthusiasm and care

He also had fun, like when he found the bonnet he decided to wear.

Not only did his hard work and dedication bring him fame

But he could also play one heck of a bridge game.

He would bid high, or pass to get out of a jam

And if he thought there was a chance, he would go for a slam.

He was unpredictable, and he didn't give a hoot

But he just didn't have much faith in a four card suit.

He will make a redoubled contract if anyone can

And talk about finesses that didn't work in the last hand.

So Butler County, we envy you in getting this hard—working, bridge—playing man

But we hope he will come back and visit the Commission whenever he can.

The person we have been talking about, as you all know, is Paul

And we just wish him best of luck in his future work, that's all!

KS 3 - 79

To Terry and Linda

Be it known that from the Campbell household
That Terry and Linda really should be told
That the St. Luke Church appreciates them very much
For all their years of service and the many lives they did touch
Terry was our treasurer for many, many years
And when money was short, he experienced all the fears
Terry directed our choir with a great deal of care
He kept cool, even when a choir member fell off a chair
He always directed with a smile on his face
Even though at times he was short a tenor and a base
And Linda too was always busy as a bee
Mother, Sunday school superintendent, children choir, she did all three
The children choir for her was a special delight
The children loved her and practiced with all their might
So, for a family that has given so much, what can one say
Except thank you so much, thanks in every way
And good luck to you both in your new home and church plan
And please come back and visit St. Luke's, whenever you can

KS 1981

Be What Makes You Happy

I am not a poet

Even though I don't know it.

But I like to play with rhymes and verses

And sometimes it really brings some curses.

You see, my father was a farmer, so I too chose that occupation

Because that's what most people were, including all of my relation

But soon, boredom set in don't you see

And I decided to try my luck at the university.

I thought I wanted to be an attorney at law, but analyzing facts was my flaw

So, I pursued economics as a plan B and found it was right up my alley

I was graduated along with the rest of the mob

And then began looking feverously for a good job.

Now, I am what they call a planner of resources

And at time, it seems as difficult as farming a year with horses.

But I have discovered it doesn't matter what you want to do or be

As long as while doing it, you can be relatively happy.

So, I will continue writing my poetry for a buffer

And let the poor reader . . . just plain suffer.

KS 1- 79

One of the Best Gifts a Father Ever Had

On October 7, 1961, something special happened
That made me shout with glee.
A beautiful baby, my one and only daughter,
Was given to me.

The one most responsible for giving me
This very special life,
Was of course my partner, my lover,
My faithful companion, yes, my wife.

My son and I had gone to the hospital
To get them after a short stay,
But all they wanted to know at the hospital was
How are you going to pay?

For we were farmers without insurance
Or extra money lying around
Because it was all invested in livestock
And in the tilling of the ground.

About then my son pipes up
Just by chance
Dad, my new sister,
Will she wet her pants?

When we got home, back to the farm,
My daughter began to grow like the dickens

She loved to help do chores, feed the cows,
And especially hug the chickens.

Now my daughters has grown into a beautiful young woman
And has a wonderful husband by her side.
Which makes us realize that life passes by rather quickly,
It is a fact that we can not hide.

But she will always be something very special
Which not at all makes me sad,
Because a daughter like her is
One of the best gifts a father ever had.

KS 2 - 87

Remembering the Forgotten Mechanic

Through the history of world aviation
Many names have come to the fore . . . .
Great deeds of the past in our memory
will last,
As they're joined by more and more . . . .
When man first started his labor in his
quest to conquer the sky
He was designer, mechanic and pilot.
And he built a machine that would fly . . . .
But somehow the order got twisted,
And then in the public's eye
The only man that could be seen
Was the man who knew how to fly . . . .
The pilot was everyone's hero.
He was brave, he was bold,
he was grand.
As he stood by his battered old biplane
With his goggles and helmet in hand . . . .
To be sure, these pilots all earned it,
To fly you have to have guts . . . .
And they blazed their names in the
hall of fame
On wings with bailing wire struts . . . .
But for each of these flying heroes
There were thousands of little reknown,
And these were the men who worked on the plane
But kept their feet on the ground...

We all know the name of Lindbergh,

And we've read of his flights to fame . . . .

But think, if you can, of his maintenance man,

Can you remember his name?

And think of our wartime heroes, Gabreski,

Jabara, and Scott . . . .

Can you tell me the name of their crew chiefs?

A thousand to one you cannot . . . .

Now pilots are highly trained people,

And wings are not easily won . . . .

But without the work of the maintenance man

Our pilots would march with a gun . . . .

So when you see mighty aircraft

As they mark their way through the air.

The grease stained man with the wrench in hand

Is the man who put them there . . . .

Anonymous

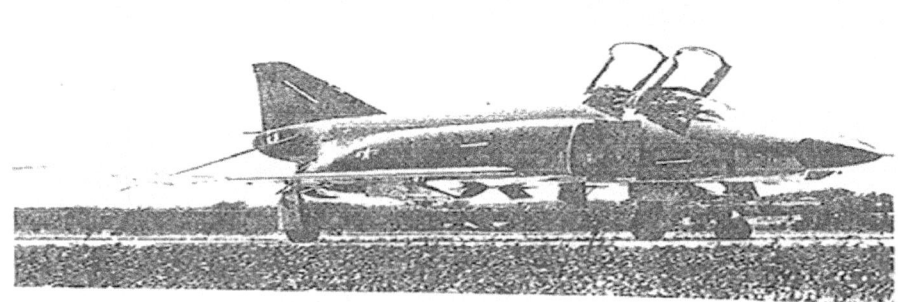

Christmas Poems

The Tree is trimmed, baking is done;
The Christmas season is here.
A special time for families,
Makes it a favorite time of year.

1991 has almost passed;
Now is the time to reminisce
With our friends and families,
Whom we dearly miss.

Keith has a new hobby,
Our friends from the fifties could guess;
Studebaker and Oliver models,
Sometimes keeps the house a mess

Maryalice still looks forward to Mondays,
As teaching is a challenge indeed;
There is always plenty of children,
That have a very special need.

Jim and Wendy keep very busy,
Being foster parents and each with a full time job.
Veronica is almost seven and in the second grade,
Healthy and full of energy, now five, is Bob.

Marla and Terry's family has grown by one;
On January 27, Kyra joined the clan.

Micah now, two and a half, at first had her doubts;
But now is her new sister's greatest fan.

In the Navy
Bill has found his place;
Fulfilling his life-long dream,
Of being a flying ace.

Camping, dancing, playing bridge,
Being grandparents, are just a few
Of the relaxing things,
That we find time to do

In closing, let us not forget,
What Christmas is celebrated for;
Christ was born to save mankind.
And through him is the open door

Merry Christmas and Happy New Year

Keith, Maryalice

Written by Maryalice in 1991

Holiday Greetings from the Sheets

It was right after Thanksgiving,
And panic had set in.
Less than thirty days until Christmas,
And I was just ready to begin.

The hustle and bustle
Of our daily grind,
Makes it hard to have
Christmas on our mind.

The malls are packed,
The shelves are getting bare,
The grandkids gave me a list,
But I don't know where.

Sugarplums are still a vision,
But the house is taking shape.
Our holiday wishes to our friends,
We don't want to be late.

Maryalice's mother broke a hip,
And needed some tender loving care.
Keith's mom is doing very well,
In September he made a trip there.

Jim's family is growing up.
This year "He" will be forty.
It doesn't seem that long ago,
Since our family began—Lordy, Lordy!

Marla's family is close by.
Her daycare keeps them busy.
We see them quite often.
The girls' activities keep us all in a tizzy.

Bill is still in the navy,
So far from us they stay.
We get to see them now and then,
When we can find a way.

The babies are becoming little ladies,
Well—Most of the time.
It is fun comparing the three of them,
And seeing what's on their mind.

Our only camping trip this year,
The last of October we would go.
But Mother Nature played a trick on us,
As we had a twelve-inch snow.

When Keith retires, he will have a hobby,
Because he purchased a new toy.
An Oliver tractor with a snow blade,
Is his latest pride and joy.

This is the season to celebrate Christ's birth.
This is what Christmas is all about.
Glory to God in the Highest,
We really want to shout.

We look forward to hearing from you.
Once a year to communicate is not much.
But to hear about your family.
Let us, at least, keep in touch.

Maryalice and Keith

MQS December 1997
Written by Maryalice 1997

To My Darling Husband on His Retirement Day

This is the day we have waited for,
Now we can spread our wings and soar.

Our plans will now be complete,
We can start on our new retreat.

Our daily schedule will begin,
Never to hear the alarm again.

First we will start with our travels,
To see the capitols and God and man-made marvels.

What lies ahead we do not know,
To touch some lives we want to grow.

We will welcome each new day,
And let the Lord lead the way.

Come along, grow old with me, the best is yet to be—

Written by Maryalice 1999

Retirement Day

Retirement Day—you say? Oh!
How can that Be?
It was always so far away,
To finally be a reality.

The road has been long and sometimes a test,
Milking cows on the farm was not my dream.
But sometimes things work out for the best,
To Lincoln we came, and life was redeemed.

As fate would have its turn,
I stumbled into a new career . . . .
Helping children to learn,
For which I was sincere.

There were students with special needs,
Some wanting knowledge, others already defeated.
I hope within I planted the smallest of seeds,
To help them see their goals completed.

For the many friendships, we are blest.
And today tears will shed
I'm looking to family, travels, hobbies, and rest
And new opportunities which lie ahead.

Written by Maryalice Quig Sheets

For her retirement May 26 reception 1999

Our Great Creator

The sun appears to come up
And it appears to go down,
But actually the whole world
Is turning around and around.

Really, our entire galaxy
Is drifting in space.
To know these kind of things,
Truly gives us the faith.

No matter if you are from
America, England, or France,
How could anyone think
This all happened by chance?

Regardless of where you live,
Or your place of birth,
Thank GOD for the life he gave,
On this spaceship called Earth

2002 KS

A Note from Heaven

What's another six months or even a year,
When the alternative is living up here?

I had a good time down there on earth,
Now it's time to move on, just like it was at birth.

We are reluctant sometimes, a fact we cannot hide,
But I did want to see loved ones, that have passed to the other side.

As it says in the good book, there is a time to live and a time to die,
A time for everything, a time to laugh and a time to cry.

It is all part of God's wonderful plans,
If we have the faith to put it in His Loving hands.

Written when my Mom passed In November 2002 KS

ODDS AND ENDS

Crucial for man is his attitude toward failure: whether it remains hidden from him and overwhelms him only objectively at the end, or whether he perceives it unobscured as the constant limit of his existence; whether he snatches at fantastic solutions and consolations or faces it honestly, in silence before the unfathomable.

The way in which man approaches his failure determines what he will become.

Geoffrey J. Warnock

1923

A fool thinks of himself as a wise man

But a wise man knows of himself to be a fool.

Approximate quote from Shakespeare

Prudent keep their knowledge to themselves but a fool's heart blurts out folly

Proverbs 12:23

We must never settle for the status quo. Our goals in life should be just out of reach—not too far, lest we become discouraged, not close, lest we become complacent.

Clayton Yeutter

1965

Nothing in the world can take the place of persistence.

Talent will not—nothing is more common than unsuccessful men with talent.

Genius will not—unrewarded geniuses are almost like a proverb.

Education will not—the world is full of educated derelicts.

Persistence and determination are omnipotent.

Benjamin Franklin

Whether ours shall continue to be a government of laws and not of men is now for congress and ultimately for the American people to decide.

(A statement made by special prosecutor Archibald Cox after President Nixon had him fired)

1973

Is a societies level of civilization measured by what it does to its criminals?

(Author unknown)

"O, I know in my heart, in the sun—quickened, blossoming soul of me This something called self is a part, but the world is the whole of me."
From "April Theology"

"Death cannot rob me of life. I've already
lived it. To grow old is the feeling you have been
fulfilled. You need not be afraid of death. I believe
It's the most wonderful experience of
Life"

John G. Neihardt

With President's Day coming and Martin Luther King Jr.'s birthday just past, we should "Thank God" for men like George Washington and Martin Luther King Jr. We should thank God that we live in a country where we are free. Free to thank God for the freedoms we have. Free to read that the Father of our country George Washington, prayed to God before he crossed the Delaware River and defeated the enemy who greatly out—numbered Washington's brave young troops. Troops willing to give their lives for freedom. Theirs and other victories gave us the freedoms we enjoy today. Freedom to exchange money that says "In God We Trust." Freedom to say "One Nation Under God" in our pledge of allegiance to our flag, that is still allowed in our schools. The freedoms of speech and press, that are guaranteed to us in our Constitution, have allowed brave men like Martin Luther King Jr. to say "Free at last, free at last, thank God almighty we are free at last." These freedoms must be preserved in places like our work areas and schools for us to stay a free nation.

Written for the "opinions" section of the Lincoln Newspaper.

KS 2000

Loyd Elmer Sheets

Loyd Sheets was born eight miles North West of Cawker City Kansas on December 3, 1909. It was stormy that day. The snow blizzard was so bad that the doctor had trouble getting to the home to assist in his birth. For his younger life see the write-up on David Sheets. In 1926, the family left Kansas and moved to the Nebraska Sandhills. Potatoes were their first crop in the Sandhills but they had mostly cattle because it was ranching country.

In 1930 Loyd married Irene Mae Knoll. They had 4 children, Bob, Dean, Keith and Gloria. In 1936 Loyd and his family moved to a farm 5 miles south of Arnold Nebraska. That is where they were living when I was born. In 1939, we moved to a farm Dad had bought five miles north of Arnold. He farmed with horses until tractors become available. His first tractor was a model B John Deere which he bought around 1940. His second tractor was a Z Minneapolis Moline. After World War II farm machinery was hard to get. In 1945 Dad found a U Minneapolis Moline for sale near St. Joseph Missouri. He bought it and drove it home. He said it was a long tractor ride but nothing like the Kansas to Nebraska cattle drives were when he was younger. In 1947, Dad bought a farm machinery store in Arnold. I helped him operate it for a few years after I got out of High School. Also in 1947 Dad rented a farm about thirteen miles west of Arnold. Our family moved to that farm and lived there several years. We farmed about two thousand acres including the home place 5 miles north of Arnold. Our crops were about one half corn and one half summer fallow wheat.

In 1949, there was a severe snow blizzard. Some of our livestock died in the blizzard. The roads were blocked for several days at a time. Sometimes we ate wild plums that Mom had canned in the fall. I also remember grinding some wheat from the grain bin to make bread.

In 1955, irrigation was installed on the farm and Loyd and his family moved irrigation pipe by hand for several years. In about 1961, Loyd sold the farm machinery store in Arnold. In about 1969, Loyd and Irene sold their farm north of Arnold. After doing some traveling, they bought and moved on to some land in Truth or Consequences, New Mexico. They live next to the Rio Grande River and enjoy fishing and gardening to this day.

KS 1985

David Elmer Sheets

David was born in Clarke County Iowa on October 25, 1877. He was the youngest in his family. David's Mother died in about 1883 when David was about 6 years old. His dad, John, died around 1890 after John and David had moved to Kansas (See write-up on John). David was only about eleven or twelve years old when his Dad died, so David lived with his sister Ester for two years. After that, he worked out as a hired man for some people in the Downs, Cawker City area.

In 1899 he married Clara Alice Burden. They had 5 sons, Claude, Merle, Wiley, Loyd, (my Dad), and Harold.

David and his sons farmed several hundred acres of land (about eight hundred I think). David had acquired some land and the remainder he rented. Of course, all the farming was done with horses. Some of the years, about five or six, when winter feed was inadequate in Kansas, David and his sons drove their cattle and some neighbor's cattle to the Nebraska Sandhills to winter them. They drove them to Blaine County near Brewster. Hay and grass were plentiful in that area as was typical for the Sandhills. One year they drove horses and cattle mixed which proved to be more difficult than driving cattle alone because the horses would run ahead and scatter the cattle. The drive would take about ten to fifteen days. My dad said it took about three days to get used to being in a saddle every day and then the rest of the trip was more bearable.

In about 1926, David moved his family to Blaine County Nebraska and ranched in the area for several years.

In 1942, he moved to a farm five miles south of Arnold Nebraska where he lived the remainder of his life farming and ranching. On holidays the Sheets families would usually gather at Dave and Alice's home there five miles south of Arnold.

David died in the Calloway hospital, due to heart problems, on June 23 1955. Alice stayed on the farm and managed the lands they had acquired until her death, also at the Calloway hospital, on May 11, 1965. Their graves are in the Arnold cemetery in the center eastwardly area.

KS 7 - 3 - 82

John Sheets

John was born in 1841 in Ohio. John served in the Civil war on the union side but as of this date I have not found his military records. He married Mary Elizabeth Butts (daughter of George W. Butts) in 1863 at Morrow County Ohio. They had five children, Mary A, Everett, Ester, Jessie and David. It appears on Census film that Mary A. was born in Illinois about 1864. They could have been on their way to Clarke County Iowa where the rest of the children were born. Elizabeth died about 1883. John remarried. When David (my Grandfather) was about nine years old (around 1886) John and his family, except for Mary and the second wife, left Iowa, and went to Kansas. John was a one-armed man. He lost his hand from a shot gun blast in a runaway, so some say. Other reports from his Grandchildren are that he just reached under the buggy seat to get his gun and it fired. John's occupation was farming. When John was about 49 years old (around 1890) he rode a horse home near Downs Kansas one day and felt a terrific pain in his side. It was an old rupture in which gangrene had set in and he died. His son David was with him when he died according to my Dad. John was buried on the Northeast side of the Downs cemetery. A grave stone was put up much later which reads "John J. Sheets 1841—1890." It also reads "Post 232 GAR"

Keith Sheets 6—10—1982

Irene Mae Knoll Sheets

Irene Sheets was born at Alton, Kansas on October 24, 1908. She was the first daughter of William and Roetta (Ulmer) Knoll. Irene had three brothers and one sisters Bill, Loyal, Irey, and Imagine. Her mom died from complications of gall bladder surgery when Irene was sixteen years old. Being the oldest child, she helped her dad raise the other children.

On November 25, 1930, she married Loyd E. Sheets (see write-up on Loyd). Irene and Loyd moved to the Arnold Nebraska area in the mid-thirties where they farmed and operated an Oliver farm implement store.

They retired in 1968 and moved to Truth or Consequence New Mexico. Loyd died on September 27, 1996. Irene stayed there until 2001 and then she moved to Ojai California to be by her daughter Gloria.

Irene died on November 12, 2002, at Ojai. Services were held at Arnold Nebraska on November 23, 2002. Interment followed the service on the Sheets plot in the Arnold Cemetery for both Irene and Loyd.

Keith Sheets August 15, 2005

SHORT
STORIES

A Christmas Visitor

It was the month of Christmas in Lincoln Nebraska and a little boy named Billy was playing in the snow in his back yard.

On this cold afternoon, Billy saw a little grey spot by the fence. It was a young field mouse that was huddled in the snow. Billy picked it up and held it in his hand. The mouse was nearly froze to death and moved very little.

Billy took the mouse in his bedroom and held it over the heat vent hoping to bring it back to life.

Billy's mother came into the room and said, "Billy what have you got in your hands?" "Billy stood up, hid the mouse in his hands and began crying. He knew his mother would make him put the mouse back outside and it would freeze to death. He ran into the kitchen. His mother followed him repeating "Billy what do you have?"

"A little mouse" Billy sobbed. "Can I keep it?"

"A mouse!" His mother screamed "No! No! you can't keep it, take it outside right now, Oh!"

Billy began crying harder. "It will freeze to death" he said. Billy's mother turned to his father and said. "What are we going to do, he wants to keep that mouse in the house!"

Billy's older brother, Jim, and sister, Marla, were shouting "let him keep it."

Billy's father was silent for a moment before he said "Why don't' we just let nature take its course?"

Billy ran down stairs and got a clear plastic box with a hole in the lid. He came back with the mouse in the box and said "We can keep him in here."

"No!" the mother said, "We can't keep a mouse in the house!"

The father said "Why don't you take it to school tomorrow and give it to your science teacher?"

Billy thought that was a good idea saying "Yeah, we had a mouse to study once before, I will take it to school."

Billy's mother reluctantly consented to let him keep the mouse to take to school. It seemed like a tentative solution to the problem and she knew how much he wanted to keep it.

Billy's father put some bread in the box and taped the lid shut. The mouse was beginning to move around more now and Billy watched it run around inside the clear plastic box. He took the box in his bedroom and set it on his dresser.

Later that evening, Billy was sitting in the hall looking real sad. "What is the matter?" his mother asks.

Billy was silent for a while and then said "I wanted to hold the little mouse in my hands again and it got away and I can't find it."

His mother looked over to the dresser to see the plastic box with the tape removed and the lid open.

Billy's sister, Marla, and father looked in all of the dresser drawers and closets in the bedroom but could not find the mouse.

"I was afraid something like this would happen" The mother said. "The mouse will probably have a family and then we will have a house full of mice."

"Two mice have to get together before they can have a family, Mom" Billy's older brother, Jim, said.

"I know!" said the mother "But maybe they have already been together."

"Maybe it's a daddy mouse" the sister said. "Besides we will find it so don't worry Mom" she added.

But they didn't find the mouse that night or the next day. It was the following evening after Billy had gone to bed when the mother noticed the family cat looking at one end of the piano. The family dog, who was smaller than the cat, was at the other end of the piano, sniffing and wagging his tail.

"There is something in the piano, it must be the mouse!" the mother said nervously.

The father moved the piano out and the mouse ran under the couch while the cat ran behind the piano.

The father moved the couch and again the cat failed to get the mouse. This time the mouse ran under the Christmas tree where all the packages were.

After they looked for some time, the mother, who was standing on a chair, said "Move that big package."

When the father moved it, the mouse ran across the floor and into the coat closet.

The mother screamed "get it" but the cat was still looking under the couch.

The father put the cat into the coat closet and shut the door. The cat caught the mouse and the father put them both out in the snow. Later the cat was let back in without the mouse.

The next day the father told Billy what happened and about the Christmas present that the cat found under the tree. He also explained that death is part of life. He ended by saying "With a slight but harmful intervention by man, I guess nature has taken its course."

Billy looked sad for a while but seemed to understand a little more about life. He had tried to help a little creature and gave it one more day of life. This seemed to be the right and proper thing to do in this Christmas season.

KS 1973

The Day Gins Died

The big sorrel horse died about one half mile west of the farm house. My father said "Gins died last night." I went to the pasture west of the house to see if it was true.

As I approached, she was lying on her side, motionless. A great contrast to the mighty body that was so active just a few years previous when she and her faithful teammate, a palomino called "Fleet" pulled the corn shucking wagon through the field. My father and my brothers would shuck the dryland corn that they had worked so hard to grow. Carefully selecting every ear, ripping off the husks with their shucking hooks and throwing it against the "back board" of the wagon. On signal, Gins and Fleet would systematically move the wagon ahead a few feet and wait for a signal to move ahead again.

So as I stood there thinking of the things Gins had done for our family I was especially sad. And other thoughts came to my mind. Like the many times my father would place me on her back and allow me to ride her to the barn, clinging to the harness.

But that was all in the past, I was old enough now to realize that she was gone forever. Also gone was the era that she lived and worked through. But she and her counterparts had played an important role in helping families like ours survive on the dry-land farms of Nebraska.

KS. 1975

The Day My Father Cried

To me, my father was the strongest man in the world—six feet, two hundred pounds, and muscles like steel. But he was strong in other ways too. For he had the grit to begin his adult life by working as a hired man and later to begin farming for himself during a very difficult period in our country—the "great depression." Of course many other men and women lived and worked during the same period. And it produced a special breed of people—a tough breed. So my Folks lived and endured life's trials.

But what was the event that could possibly make my father cry—something I thought was impossible? For it was the era that men and boys were not to cry, or show emotion. The family had traveled from the farm to the airport that special day. After the "goodbyes," we were standing watching the big plane make it's ascend and soar over our heads. I looked up at my father. He was crying. What could make this happen? The normal love of a father for his son. For you see his oldest son was flying off to the war in Korea.

KS 1975

The Great American Dessert — Legend or Reality?

In 1953, we had a partial crop only because of the subsoil moisture of previous years rains.

In 1954, we only harvested the lowlands. The remainder of the crop turned brown in August. Brown as the flesh on my father's arms. And the two are not that unrelated you see. Because it was my father's flesh, muscle, sweat and determination that had planted and cultivated each stock of corn. Corn that looked so healthy the first of July that it brought joyful exclamations like "It is going to be knee high by the 4th."

But when the hot dry south winds of August came, like they had so many years before, and turned all of the crops brown, there was little to be joyful about. Because we all knew that it would be another year of survival, of hanging on, and hoping that maybe next year we would have a good crop and plenty of feed for our livestock.

I am sure many times my father thought "God are we supposed to be trying to grow crops on this land? Or is it truly the 'Great American Desert' that the first explorers named it?"

But then in 1955, like many Nebraska farmers, we tapped the underground rain, the hidden Oasis—240 feet of well casing, an eight-inch pump and head, and a 180 horse-power motor. The water level stood at 190 feet with less than 10 foot of draw down while pumping 1000 gallons per minute. The answer to all of our problems? Not quite. For we did not know what the future held. Energy sources are not unlimited. And no water supply in the world is unlimited. So irrigators of Nebraska farms, use your water supply carefully and conservatively. Or the "Great American Desert" legend may still come true.

KS 1975

"Snortin Pole"

The "Snortin Pole," also referred to as an idiot stick by some people, was a forked stick about five feet long. It had no special operating instructions. The operator (or idiot as sometimes called) would merely unhook his end of the irrigation pipe (carefully keeping his fingers extended) and place the pipe in the fork. Then extending it above his head as far as possible, to clear the nine-feet tall corn, he would walk, or stumble through the mud about sixty feet laterally and begin hunting for the other line of pipe to hook it to. This would continue until every joint of pipe was moved, every night and morning throughout the irrigation season. It was enough to make one huff and puff. And before you were through you would surely be "snortin" too.

KS 1975

Preface

The following true story was written in February 1987 by our youngest son Bill, who was one of three special blessings God gave to us. Bill was born on September 5, 1966, nearly five years after Marla's birth and over eight years after Jim's. The two older children's birth were written about previously in this book (See "Miracles" and "One of the Best Gifts a father ever had.")

Keith and Maryalice Sheets

Cancer Story by Bill

The operator's voice sounded nasally as she spoke with a southern accent. "I have a collect call from a Mr. Bill Sheets. Will you accept the charge?" I was standing outside on the street corner hoping that I would not have to plug the payphone with quarters. "Yes, I will accept the charges." "Mom how are you?" "I'm fine, Bill. How are you?" "Great, I can't wait to get home tomorrow. I'm so excited." "I am too, Bill." Mom's voice was cold. I did not understand why she did not seem enthused to hear from me. Had she forgotten I was coming home tomorrow? I thought I would give Dad a try. Maybe he will sound a little more excited. "Mom, get Dad on the phone." "Bill, I have some bad news." I knew something was not right. "Dad had major surgery for cancer yesterday." I grabbed the steel frame of the pay phone for support. My mouth was dry. "What happened," I asked. "He went for a physical last week and the doctor found some cancerous growths in his colon. They had to operate as soon as possible."

I stared at the faded numbers on the telephone dial. My mind and body were numb from what I just heard. These things happen to other people. I wanted to hang up, call back and wish that I had just gotten the wrong number.

"Is he okay?"

"He is in stable condition." Mom proceeded to tell me all she could in the remaining minutes of our call.

Walking back to the barracks took what seemed like a life time. I should have been running for that was one of the rules the Army had given me, to run everywhere you went. But, I had forgotten about the Army and their silly games for the moment. My world was preoccupied with my dad and his condition, and how I was going to deal with the emotions I was feeling.

Once upstairs, I put my coat and hat on my desk and went to sit on my bed. Then I remembered we were not allowed to sit on our beds; just sleep in them. I sat down anyway and buried my face into my hands. I could feel the wool of the blanket pressing through my pants and itching my legs. Why couldn't the Army issue cotton blankets? I felt nausea.

Ron, a friend from Louisiana, came over and put me in a head lock and rubbed the top of my head with his knuckles.

"What is wrong," He asked. "Are you okay?" The tone of his voice projected the sincerity of his question.

As I began to tell him the news, a lump began to swell in my throat cutting off any words I tried to say. Instead of speaking, I wept. I felt Ron's hand on my shoulder holding me steady.

The next morning he drove me to the airport and made sure I got on the right flight. My seat was next to a window that overlooked the right wing. I could see men below loading luggage onto a conveyer belt that went inside the belly of the plane. I leaned my head back, put on my headphones, and listened to a Phil Collins tape. I tried to relax.

I had not been home in four months. My homecoming was supposed to be happy and exciting. There was not supposed to be any grief or hardship. Things are supposed to be perfect at Christmas time. Especially this Christmas. It would be the first time in four months I was finally going to see family.

All the time I was away from home I had built up a special feeling for going back home and seeing the people that I love so much. Now that feeling was being threatened. Would I be able to talk to Dad and tell him how much I missed him and loved him or would I be deprived of sharing those feelings with him forever. I took those feelings for granted, like so many things in life people take for granted. When they lose something or someone special it is too late to say I love you.

I heard the landing gear lower beneath me and a couple minutes later I felt the jolt of the wheels touch the ground. Coming off the plane I looked frantically for a familiar face. I spotted her. It was my girlfriend Lissy. It was good to see someone I cared about. We picked up my luggage and drove to the hospital. The sky was an overcast of light and dark grays, which I hoped would not foreshadow the near future.

Hospitals always had given me a feeling of uneasiness. Today was no exception. Lissy and I walked down the hall looking for my father's room. We stopped, wondering if we had the right floor when a voice said, "Hey there soldier." It was my mother. I turned around and gave her a hug. "Where's Dad's room" I asked. She took me to the door and I stood there a moment scared to go inside, afraid of what I might find out, afraid of having to face reality, afraid of facing life. Then I walked into the room cautiously. It smelled like Mom's medicine cabinet back home. I walked around the curtain divider and saw Dad. He looked fragile.

"Dad," I asked. He looked startled at first, then I saw a smile come across his face. He held out his hand. I went to him just like I had done as a little boy. I took his hand and held it, I noticed that my hand was larger than his now. I wished it was small again like a child.

"How are you," I asked in almost a whisper.

"I am a little sore from the surgery, but I feel fine. The doctor said they got all the cancer. He said it was a success." I hugged him and told him that I loved him. I was overwhelmed with joy. "When do you get to come home?"

"The doc said maybe before Christmas if my stitches take hold."

Dad and I talked for the rest of the afternoon. We told each other how we felt. I told him things I was never able to tell him before about my feelings for him. And he did the same.

I learned from that experience in my life, that any time something could happen to take loved ones away from you. And that the time with those loved ones is very precious; an irreplaceable moment in time and should not be taken for granted.

The Christmas turned out to be the best Christmas I ever had. The best gift of all was Dad coming home.

February 1987

Bill Sheets

LETTERS

United States Navy
Dads Military Retirement By Bill

NAS Corpus Christi
Corpus Christi, Texas

July 12, 1998

To: Marlin Keith Sheets, MSGT, USAFNG
From: Bill T. Sheets, LT, USN
Subject: *Retirement from Service*

As an officer in the United States Navy, it is an honor and pleasure to present you with this retirement Shadow Box.

The Shadow Box has a long tradition of reflecting the retiree's accomplishments throughout the serviceman's career. It is a shadow of his experiences and should be looked upon not as boasting but should instill great pride for this represents commitment, duty, and honor. Let all that look upon this box reflect what it means to be a responsible citizen of the United States of America.

Our freedoms, which so many take for granted, do not come without the few dedicated servicemen who are willing to stand the watch, willing to make sacrifices if need be, willing to leave their families in the defense of our Constitution and country if need be, and willing to give their lives if need be.

Let it be known to all men that Master Sargent Marlin Keith Sheets, United States Air Force National Guard, gave twenty—two years of faithful service to his country.

I am proud to be able to call you my father. You have instilled in me integrity, morals, values, and a sense of duty. I pray I can become half the man you are, and I may instill into my children the same set of values you have instilled in me. I also pray they may come to understand the meaning of honor, courage, and commitment. Thank you, Dad. You are my hero.

Very Respectfully,

Bill J. Sheets

Bill. T. Sheets
Lieutenant United States Navy

Dear Veronica,
To Veronica From Santa

Thank you for your continuous belief in me. I am a mythical man, the spirit of Christmas giving. I have been around for over a thousand years making children happy at Christmas, and I will continue for many more years to come for those who believe in me.

The practice of giving gifts began when the three wise men brought gifts to baby Jesus and has continued through the years.

I have many, many helpers to assist me in getting ready for the special event of Christmas.

You could say that Mrs. Claus and I have two wonderful children whom we love very much.

Thank you for your letter! I will do my best to bring the toys and gifts you have asked for. Enjoy your Christmas, which as you know is a celebration of Jesus' birth.

Merry Christmas,

Santa Claus

Written by Maryalice 1994

Dear Grandma and Granddad

From Kids and Grandkids

How are you? I'm fine. I have glasses now. I just got them. I was saling girl scout cookies. I sold thirty-eight boxes. I was short one Savannah. During a blizzard I worked on my scout, and I have two badges done.

They are "pets" and "drawing" and "painting."

In school, in science, we are studying about smoking and drugs. In geography, we are studying about Africa.

Our block has lots of kids. There is one fourth grade on my block. Mommy burned her leg. She was boiling eggs and spilled it on her leg. Sorry, I didn't write sooner. Bye now.

Love,

Marla

Written in 1970 by Marla, (age eight) while the family was living in Lexington, Nebraska.

Are Mothers are sweet, they taught us to eat. They gave us there love it came from above. We all love are mothers, they are very nice lovers, you miss them so much when they go, but you have to go on with the flow. But you'll always have them in your heart.

Written and read by Jacey Sheets (age seven) at her great Grandma Sheet's funeral on November 2002

Hidden

Can you see it in me?
The things I try to hide.
Far beneath the smiles
Of my pretty face,
Underneath is a secret place.
It's place you do not know,
Who has never seen the world.
A secret place of thoughts
I can't bare to show.
When you look at me what do you see?
Nothing but a little girl,
Afraid to tell it all.
But if you get to know,
And if you dare to care,
You will find my hidden place,
Full of love to share

By Micah Kurtenbach, 2002 (age thirteen)

b.t.sheets@worldnet.att.net

o52tractor@aol.com

Hey guys,

Just thought I would share Jacey's latest poem. She wrote this for a teacher of hers in Pennsylvania that just had a baby.

"It's A Joyful Day"
By Jacey Sheets, second grader

It's a joyful day
Your new baby is here to stay!
Cute and cuddly moments are starting today!
With her crib all full of love.
She came from heaven up above.
It's a happy day
And it will stay!

Pretty amazing, huh. Talk to you later. Love, Bill

b.t.sheets@worldnet.att.net

o52tractor@aol.com

Hey Mom,

Here is the latest poem that Jacey created on her own.

"*Courage*" by Jacey Sheets

A little sparkle in the sky yelled down,

"Courage, courage!"

I asked, "What is courage?'

He said, "Courage is a star that sparkles bright and it even lights up the night."

You can never see that bravery that shines in you.

You have to find it yourself but, everybody has it.

That is all about courage.

Pretty amazing that a seven—year—old has a big picture that take some adults all their lives to realize. This is your granddaugther.

Talk to you later. Bill

LIFE'S
MEMORIES

Letter To The Kids

Hi Kids,

Keith's

I hope you don't mind being called "kids." Let me say to that, the older your Mom, Maryalice, and I get, the better that word "kids" sounds when someone calls us that. Not that you aren't worthy to be called children. We love every one of you—nothing will ever change that.

Well, I am finally going to get started on this writing down past memories that you Kids have asked for. Jim gave us books that prompted us to write about our past but we never filled them in—thanks anyway Jim. Marla has asked too (I think). And Bill has been after us for some time to do it. Before we get done, you might be sorry you asked. Maryalice said she might write some about her childhood and life later for you too. So we are going to start thinking on it some and see what happens. Maybe we should wait another ten years or so or until we forget some more of the stuff. Just remember, you asked for it. I have told some of you that the amount of changes in your life time will probably be more than the changes we have seen in our lifetime. So you better start thinking about writing them down for your Kids to have someday. The outline is nearly completed now and this is just going to be some of the stories and incidents that I think may have interest for you. Anyway here it goes and I will try not to use the "I" word too much so bear with me.

Early Childhood

I was born, Marlin Keith Sheets, on July 24, 1937, at the Hospital in Arnold Nebraska to Irene (Knoll) Sheets and Loyd E. Sheets. At that time, we were living five miles south of Arnold in a farm house on a hill. I can't remember anything about living there. Later, we moved to a farm five miles north of Arnold where I spent most of my childhood years. I had very good parents and like most parents, they lived, worked and would do almost anything for their Kids. I guess that is what a lot of life is about—getting your kids and grandkids raised up and started off on living a good life of their own.

I had two older brothers, Bob and Dean; and later a younger sister, Gloria. My folks would spank us kids if we needed it. Dad did most of the spanking and sometimes he would use a leather strap or a belt. It hurt but he would usually stop not too long after we started crying. So we soon learned to cry early in the spanking. If we tried to be tough and not cry, then it would be a longer ordeal than we bargained for. His parents spanked him. I heard him tell many times that his Mother had used a thorny rose bush one time to get his attention. But Grandma said she never hurt him that bad.

One of the first things that I can remember was a spanking that came from my Mother. It was before I was old enough to go to school but I had visited school to see what it would be like. I think I was about four years old at the time. However, when school was let out, I didn't go home. I went on by home to the neighbor's place to play with the little neighbor girl— Ginger was her name. By the time I did get home, it was getting late. Mom was down on her hands and knees scrubbing the kitchen floor with a wooden scrub brush. When I walked in to the kitchen, she said "Where have you been"? And she warmed my little bottom good with that wooden scrub brush. I think it may have hurt just as much as a rose bush would have. I know it left an imprint on my memory, but after that I always told her where I was going and when I might be home. Maryalice said the only spanking she can remember getting was when she was a little girl at Arnold, she was playing out in the middle of the street making the cars stop for her or running out of the way at the last minute. Her dad wasn't impressed. Anyway, those were different times. I am glad you Kids use time outs, withholding privileges, and other means of disciplining your kids. It can be just as effective if used right but I guess an occasional swat, when they are little, may not hurt anything either. As Grandparents, we are not alone in wishing we had a second chance to raise our Kids after we have lived many years and supposedly got wise about some things. Enough about that.

The following year when I started school, I liked it very much. We walked to and from school which was only about one mile and not uphill both ways. It was a one room school house. I did not have a classmate all through grade school but of course did in high school. Being the only one in my class, I got one on one attention from my teacher when it was my time for a subject. In the winter, we would set closer to the wood or coal burning stove to stay warm. We did have some work books some times. My first reading book was a "See Jane——see Jane run" kind of book. Recess was a favorite time where we would play different games like hide and seek.

Another thing I can remember doing that I liked was picking wild fruit in our pasture. We lived in Mills Valley five miles north of Arnold NE for most of my childhood. The farm had about half farmland and half pastureland. The pastureland had big tree covered canyons and the cows could hide really well in them. These canyons also had all kinds of wild fruit in them that was usually ripe in late summer. Some of the fruit that I remember was chokecherries, grapes, currents, plums, mulberries, and goose berries. We would go out and pick the fruit as a family and Mom would can it for use at a later time. We usually took a picnic lunch along and it was just a fun time. We would spread a bed sheet down under the mulberry trees and us kids would crawl up in the tree and shake the branches and it would "rain" mulberries down onto the sheets for a while. Fresh mulberries with cream and sugar sure are good. Most of the wild fruit was really good to eat but if you ate too much of it, look out. It could be pretty powerful—I will talk more about that later. Mom also canned lots of wild plums. One time we were picking plums by a highway and every once in a while one of us kids would throw wild plums at a passing car. Not a good thing to do so don't try it. Maybe because of weed spray or something else, there just isn't much wild fruit anymore.

The next thing I want to tell you about my childhood is when we would go to town on Saturday nights. We would usually go to town every Saturday night to sell cream that had been separated from milk (more about that later) and to buy groceries. To get ready to go to town, we all had to have our weekly bath. Mom would get out the old galvanized wash tub (a metal tub about twice the size as a bushel basket) for this occasion. She would heat water on her cob/wood burning cook stove and pour some in the tub. Then us kids each got our turn in the tub. She would always say "be sure to wash your neck and behind your ears." And if you didn't, she would do it for you and usually not too gently. Usually, there was no changing of the water so the first kid got the cleanest bath. Sometimes, if we were extra dirty she would change the water one time but it all had to be carried in from outside, heated on the stove, and poured into the tub. Sometimes, I think of those times while I am in the shower every morning and just count my blessing that times have changed for the better. My Dad used to tell us that "cleanness is next to Godliness" so later in life when we got running hot water and a real bath tub, we bathed EVERY day and enjoyed it.

After we all got ready, we would load up in the 1941 Ford pickup and head for town. There was one rough bridge and some corners on the way to town, so us boys would ride in the back of the pickup and hold on to the cream cans so they wouldn't upset and spill the cream. Once in town (a five-mile trip) the first stop was the creamery where they tested the cream for butter fat and gave us money for groceries and etc. While Mom and Dad were buying groceries and supplies, us kids would usually just walk back and forth up and down main street watching people. One time we were following some cowboys that were walking along with their hands stuck in their back pockets. One of my brothers said "let's do the same with our hands." So I walked up behind the cowboys and started to put my hands in their back pockets until I was stopped by my brothers. This is what they told me—I was young enough that I don't remember it too well. But I always had a way of taking things very literally or in the wrong way (more about that later too.) Sometimes we would get around early and go to a movie on Saturday nights. Yes, they were talking movies but just in black and white. The movies always started with a serial (kind of like a soap opera) that was continued from week to week to encourage people to come back every week to see what would happen. This was followed by the main feature. We often saw western movies starring Roy Rogers or Gene Autry which are probably two people you have never heard of but they were the heroes of our younger days. I also remember seeing "Gone with the Wind" staring Clark Gable in the mid 1940's. I remember that my Dad missed some of it because he had to take my baby sister out for a while because she was crying. It was a long four-hour movie about the civil war as most of you probably know. They still might be showing it today as it was a very popular movie. Well, that is probably enough about Saturday nights. Candy bars, pop, and popcorn were about five cents—those were the days.

Before Electricity

Now I want to tell you what it was like before we had electricity on our farm. You kids can write about what it was like before computers and cell phones but I will write about the "Before Electricity" era.

The first radio in the home that I can remember was a battery powered one. We would gather around it in the evenings and listen to programs like "Fibber Magee and Molley, Amos and Andy, Bob Hope, Red Skeleton, Intersanctum," etc. I have heard that you can still get some of these programs on the new satellites radios, so check them out.

The lamps we used were either white gas with a mantle or coal oil with just a wick. Of course they both had the glass chimneys. The gas lamp gave the best light for reading and other things. It was more of a white light where the coal oil lamp was more yellow. If the wick was turned too high, the coal oil lamp would smoke up its chimney. We would carry the lamps to different rooms of the house as needed but had to be careful not to drop or upset them.

With no electric pumps, the water for home use had to be pumped with a hand pump and then carried into the house. Some of the homes had a hand pump inside of the house and some had gravity water pressure from a cistern on a nearby hill or an elevated supply tank.

For keeping things cool in the summer time, several different creative methods were used. We would put jars of milk in an outside barrel of water. The barrel was wood with metal rings around it and the water would stay cool in it. We also had an ice box that could keep things cool when ice was available. Getting ice for the ice box was quite a chore sometimes too. Mom also canned a lot of fruits and vegetables as a way of preserving them for later use. Sometimes we would hang meat outside in the winter time to keep it from spoiling (butchering for the meat in the first place is another story in itself). Of course the meat had to be hung high enough that some hungry animal couldn't reach it. Later, when we got our first gas refrigerator, keeping our food preserved was a lot easier. To keep ourselves cool in the summertime we would sometimes get into a clean stock tank and play around.

Now keeping things warm in the winter called for more creative ideas. We often sat around the kitchen stove which burned wood, coal, corn cobs, and yes sometimes even cow chips too. Gathering fuel for the stoves was another chore with a lot of potential stories too. Getting up out of a warm bed in the mornings to build fires in the stoves was a memorable experience too. We had a "potbellied" stove in the living room closer to the bedrooms. We didn't try to keep the stoves burning all night so sometimes it would get pretty cold before morning came. These kind of nights took a lot of covers on the bed to stay warm. I did have somewhat of an advantage by sleeping between two big brothers and a dog. I don't ever remember getting too cold in bed. Sometimes Mom would give us hot flat irons or bricks that we could put in bed with us. We usually wore our "long john" underwear to bed also. In the mornings, however, after we got the potbellied stove fired up, you didn't want to back up too close to the stove (especially with your "barn door" down) or you might get your bottom burned. That had been known to happen occasionally. That about does it for this chapter. Now we will move on to "Doing Chores."

Doing Chores

They could be kind of dreaded words "doing chores" around the farm because they always had to be done morning and night. This kept one tied down to being at the farm every day. When we were able to get a way for a short vacation, we would have to find someone to do the chores while we were gone and sometimes that was difficult to do. The chores did not always get done right while we were away. Daily chores included feeding livestock and for us always milking cows so that we could sell the cream for grocery money.

Before we could milk the cows, we had to go get them from the pasture. Being the youngest boy, this was usually my job. We had a big pasture with several tree studded canyons where wild fruit grew and cows could hide. Sometimes I would try to catch a horse to ride but since that in itself could be a big job (more about that later), I would usually just walk after the cows.

Walking after the cows proved to be interesting at times. One time while walking, I heard a high shrill cry coming from the path ahead of me. It was a little rabbit being squeezed to death by a large bull snake. I took a stick and tried to hit the snake to make it release its prey. The snake let out a loud hiss that scared me into just leaving it alone to enjoy its meal. I did not (and still do not) like snakes. We had both rattlesnakes and bull snakes on the farm and this was my first encounter that I can remember with a bull snake. One that I never forgot.

Another time after I had found the cows and was walking along behind them, I saw something flopping around on the path. It was a hen pheasant that the cows had stepped on. It died so I took it home and Mom fried it for our supper that evening. It was good eating but I always was careful about following the cows on foot after that. I couldn't help thinking that if that had been a rattlesnake the cows stepped on, he would have been plenty mad by the time I walk up on him.

The last story I want to tell you about going after cows involves my two big brothers. They had found a can of Half and Half (brand name) tobacco on a farm we had rented west of Arnold. And while they were finding the tobacco, I was with Mom picking rhubarb that was growing around the farmstead. She would use it to make pies and jelly. I would pick some and also eat some of it raw. Before we were done, I had eaten much (too much) raw rhubarb. After we got home my brothers had stoked up a corn cob pipe and were smoking that old tobacco. They told me it was time for me to head out after the cows. I agreed to only if they let me smoke their pipe, which they did. After a few big drags from the pipe, I began walking after the cows but didn't get very far before feeling very sick. My stomach was queasy, I was in a cold sweat but did begin to feel better after upchucking the raw rhubarb that I had eaten earlier. That was something I never forgot, but I never ate raw rhubarb or even smoked too much tobacco after that unforgettable incident. Next, I will tell you some stories about milking the cows.

Milking cows was always one of the main chores to be done. The first that I can remember about milking cows was before we even had stanchions to hold them. We would take our milk bucket and stool out to the corral and follow a cow around until you got her in a corner or someplace where she would stand for milking. Often times near the end of the milking while stripping her out, your hand would slip off of the teat and hit the bucket making a noise. This would scare the cow and she would leave the scene requiring you to follow her around again to get her to stand for the last bit of stripping. In the winter time we would milk the cows in the open area of the horse barn. If your hands got cold you could slip them up between the cow's leg and her udder for a nice hand warming and she would usually stand for that. Later, Dad built some stanchions to hold the cows for milking. Some cows were harder to milk than others and we would all take our turns on the hard to milk ones. It was a time to talk, squirt milk into a cat's mouth or do other things to make it more enjoyable. Later in life after I married your Mother (the city girl), I taught her to milk. She says it was the biggest mistake she ever made to let me teach her to milk. But look at the experiences she would have missed out on. All of the cows had names and she liked the cows most of the time. However, she did learn how to swear some during this time of her life, especially if a cow stepped on her foot or slapped her in the face with a dirty tail. It was during cow milking that we discussed different things and even decided on the names of you kids.

After the cows were milked, they were released back out into the corral to eat hay and etc. Sometimes, just for fun, we would ride the cows out of the barn for a mini rodeo. One time my brothers decided it would be fun to saddle some cows to make them easier to ride. Your Uncle Dean got bucked off of one and landed on his spurs which punctured one cheek of his bottom. He never tried that again. One other time my two brothers thought it would be fun to tie two cows tails together before turning them out of the stanchions. They did this and the cows begin pulling against each other. They thought this was funny until one of the cows tail end was pulled off leaving her with a short tail. Then they begin to think what Dad was going to say or do when he found out what happened. They thought they would get the belt for sure but Dad never did figure out just what had happened. They buried the end of the tail. When Dad asked what happened to that cow's tail, they said they didn't know. They said maybe worms ate it off. I don't think Dad believed that "tale" but nothing more was ever said about it and my brothers never got the whipping they had feared.

After the cows were turned out of the barn, the barn door had to be shut. The barn door was a big door hung on a sliding rail. It was really hard to push it shut and it took both of my brothers pushing on it to get it to slide shut. I used to wait until the door was just about shut and then run through the narrow opening before it was completely shut—thinking this was a lot of fun. Well, one time I miss judged the distance and it caught me right on both sides of my head. Boy did that smart and I don't think I have ever been quiet right since—at least that is my excuse. I did notice the pain right away and the memory of it has never left me.

After the milk was carried to the milk house, we began cranking it through the separator to get the cream separated from the skim milk. The cream would be put in a can for Saturday night groceries and the skim milk would be carried out and fed to the pigs or claves. We didn't have any nipple buckets so a newly born calf would have be taught to drink milk from a bucket. This proved to be quite interesting at times. One would begin this chore by first getting the calf to start sucking your fingers. Then you pour some milk down through your fingers and then shove his nose down into the milk pail hoping he would begin the drinking process. This would usually take a while with some spilt milk, bit fingers, bunting, swearing and yes sometimes getting mad and slapping the poor little calf a few times. My description doesn't do the process justice so I will quit there. It is one of those things that is hard to describe and you just have to experience it.

When a cow delivered a new calf, we would let the new calf suck his mother's milk for about a week before taking him from her and keeping her milk. The cows would get quite creative when they knew this was going to happen. Sometimes, they would hide their new born calves from us. One time when we were sure a cow had "come fresh" or delivered a calf, we couldn't find the calf. We had looked all over the pasture and every hiding place we could think of. I did notice that she would spend time at a certain place in the pasture near the fence line that separated the pasture from a wheat field. We found out that she would send her calf through the fence into the waist high wheat to lay down and hide during the day. At night she would call it to her side for feeding. This went on for about a week before we could figure out what was happening. And they call them "dumb animals"?

A little later in life on the farm, Jim and Marla (Bill came after we left the farm) would help us by feeding the cows a can of soybean meal on top of the grain in front of the stanchions. It was kind of interesting because some of the cows would bunt Marla as she poured the soybean meal on the grain. We didn't know why they did this. I think that is about enough of chore stories for now. Now we want to talk about some farm bulls.

Bulls

Most of our milk cows were Holsteins that Dad had hauled out of Wisconsin as babies. Instead of getting more Wisconsin baby calves for replacements, Dad purchased Holstein bulls to produce the replacements and increase the herd size. Holstein bulls had kind of a reputation for being mean and ornery which leads to some of the following bull stories.

Some of my first memories of encounters with bulls was with a little bull calf we had named "Tuffy." We were still milking outside without stanchions and while carrying two pails of milk across the corral, Tuffy would bunt you from behind and sometimes cause you to spill the milk. When he was small, it was kind of cute but he soon began to grow bigger. He was not very big yet when he bunted my arm up against a big nail on the side of the barn. I still have the scar on my wrist from that "cute trick." When the bulls became full grown, they were to be respected and feared if one planned on living to enjoy old age. Usually they would do a lot of pawing, bellowing and bowing their neck as a bluff before they actually charged at you. You never quite knew when they were just bluffing or were ready to charge. One time my uncle went to the pasture to check the stock tank for water and the bull was there at the tank. As my uncle approached the tank, the bull began his bluffing act and started towards my uncle. My uncle said he picked up a nearby brick and hurled it hard, hitting the on—coming bull in the middle of the forehead. He said the brick broke into several pieces but the bull kept coming forward. My uncle said he decided it was more than a bluff so he left the scene and just assumed there was some water in the stock tank. I think it was that same bull that chased me out of the corral at a later time. I must have had a temporary lack of sanity and was trying to out bluff the bull with a big stick. I backed him half way across the corral before he charged and put me under the fence in a big hurry. I didn't know I could run and slide under a fence as fast as I did that day—something I never forgot and I am glad I lived to tell you about it.

The next bull story was after I was married and was hauling a bull back from where I had bought him in Ravana NE. We (a friend of mine and I) were about one half the way home when the back wheel of my 1954 Ford pickup came off. I was able to steer it to the side of the road without upsetting and losing the bull. I was a little concerned that the bull might try to climb out over the top of my pickup stock racks but he seemed okay after we got stopped—just a little nervous. We didn't know what to do, so after getting the wheel back on with just two lug bolts holding, we slowly drove to a nearby town and called my brother Bob. He came with his large stock truck and we drove my pickup (bull and all) into the back of his stock truck and headed for home. The bull in the pickup and the pickup in the stock truck was a rare sight to say the least. After stopping at a couple of small town bars to calm our nerves, it was after dark when we finally did get home. Then we had to figure out how to get the bull unloaded from the lofty place he had been for several hours. We finally found a ditch bank high enough to unload the pickup and then unload the bull. When I opened the pickup tailgate, the bull was in such a hurry to get out that he squeezed me up against the side of the chute on his way out. But again I survived and lived to tell about it.

The last bull story that I will punish you with was also after being married and was farming with your uncle Dean. On the farm, it was necessary to keep the bulls separated from the cows until a selected time. This way the baby calves would be born during the time of your choosing, weather wise and etc. But this one bull kept getting in with the cows and we didn't know how he was able to since no fence was down or gates open. We finally figured out that he was walking through the stock tank which was located between the two corrals. So Dean suggested stringing an electric wire from our "weed burner" fencer across the middle of the tank to put a stop to the bull's adventures. We surmised that the scene might be worth watching so we opened a crack in the barn door to see through and waited for the bull to try it one more time. He started wading through the water and the electric wire was under his belly, back just about where the body parts start getting real tender when the first jolt of electricity hit him. Standing in water, he was getting the maximum amount of electricity the fencer had. He stopped and let out a loud bellow and backed up a little. But thinking about the prize and all the fun with the cows on the other side of the tank, he had started forward again when the second jolt of electricity hit him. He let out another bellow and decided it wasn't going to be worth it and backed out of the stock tank. We never found him over with the cows after that until later in the year when we opened the gate for him. I think it was kind of a hard lesson for him though. Enough bull for one time. Next we want to talk about horses on the farm.

Horses

Horses played a very important part on the farms before tractors became plentiful (see "The Day Jins Died" previously written). In addition to helping with the field work, we would occasionally use them to help get the cows in from the pasture—if we could catch a horse to ride. We had this one old saddle horse called "Spot." Spot was a nice gentle horse but he was also kind of lazy. He would do all kinds of things to keep from being caught and ridden after the cows. I would walk out into the horse corral and if I had the bridle in my hands, he would run away from me. Sometimes I could get him into a corner of the corral and get the bridle on him but it was a job that could take a considerable amount of time. For that reason, I would usually walk after the cows and hope they were not too far over the hills to find. Later we got another saddle horse called "Bill" and he was much easier to catch and ride. Sometimes we would ride the horses to school, especially after we moved to the farm west of Arnold where the school was about two miles from home. There was a barn on the school grounds to keep the horses in during school time. The barn was also good for games like "Hide and Seek." I think my brothers rode horses to school when we were living south of Arnold too.

One time after I was able to catch and bridle Spot, I wound up walking home after all. Spot would often shy (jump sideways) after seeing a little mound of dirt or for any other excuse he could find to unload his rider and run home. Since we usually rode bareback (no saddle), I would hold on tight to some of his mane on the top of his neck. This one particular time, I was holding on to some mane and an empty canvas water bag with the same hand. Spot shied at something. I was able to stay on him but at the end of his movement, the water bag would swing around towards his neck and he would shy again at the bag. This went on for several turns as he was shying in a circle. I was holding on very tight, determined to stay on his back. The problem was I couldn't turn loose of the water bag without losing my grip on his mane and falling off. After several circles and much laughter from my brothers who were watching this all take place, I did release the water bag and yes, the bag and I both fell to the ground. I got up and said "well I could see he wasn't going to stop, so I thought I better get off." My brothers laughed and teased me about that incident for years to come. Being thrown from a horse was just one of those things that happened occasionally to keep one a little humble. Usually, your pride was all that was hurt. I have found in later years of life that when your ego gets a little too inflated, one of these humbling experiences come along to get you back on track. I guess that is God's way of keeping us humble. Now to get back on track with the horse stories. I know I am using the "I" word too much and my ego is probably showing through at times, but bear with me and we will get through this—one way or the other. I am not the best writer but am trying to fulfill a special request here.

The next horse story involves my brother Dean and me. My brother Bob died from a stroke at young age so Dean and I were closer as brothers. After I got married, I had a pickup and a horse of my own (we bought Jim a pony named Princess but I can't remember the name of my horse). Anyway, I drove onto the farm and Dean was west of the house chasing an uncooperative bull. I could see that Dean needed some help so I unloaded the horse, quickly threw the saddle on and started riding at a fast gallop toward Dean and the bull. As I got closer to Dean, still galloping hard, things started looking a little sideways and the saddle turned on the horse dumping me to the ground where I rolled to a stop fairly close to Dean and his horse. In My haste to saddle the horse, I had not got the saddle cinch tight enough to hold it upright for a fast gallop. It was another one of those humbling experiences and Dean was laughing and making the most of it. He found it to be very humorous. After getting myself up, dusted off and the horse resaddled, we were able to get the bull driven back to his pen at the barn. After that incident, I tried to make sure that the saddle cinches were good and tight before mounting the horse. This usually required two tries because sometimes the horses would hold their stomachs tight to make it seem like the cinch was tight when it wasn't, which leads us to the next story.

It was the spring of the year and time to move cattle to their permanent summer pasture. We had arrived at Dean's farm early in the morning. My nephew (Mike) and I were saddling the horses in preparation for the big cattle drive to the summer pastures. This was kind of a fun day where farm families got a chance to work together. My nephew saddled the horse that Dean would be riding (Dean never believed me but yes my nephew did saddle that horse). And yes, he didn't get the cinch tight enough. We were about one hour into our cattle drive and it was a constant job trying to keep the cattle from going off of the road and eating from some farmers nice green wheat field. This is what had happened and I was needing some help in trying to get the cattle back onto the road. This time, Dean saw that I needed help and began riding at a fast gallop towards me and the cows. He was riding a young colt that would stiffen his front legs and bounce real hard several times when reined up to stop. As Dean started to rein him up to slow down, the colt started his bouncing and on about the third bounce, the saddle cinch gave loose. The horse stopped and Dean and the saddle went air borne. Dean was holding on to the saddle horn and he rode that saddle through the air clear to the ground. Still in the saddle, setting on the ground with a blank look on his face, he accused me of saddling his horse. Of course I was the one laughing then, while he was accusing me of saddling his horse that morning. I told him the truth, that Mike did it but I am not sure he believes me even to this day.

Tractors

The coming of the tractor was a very big change for the farmers of our country. Like any new change, some were reluctant to accept the change and continued to use their horses for farming. They claimed that the tractors would compact the ground too much. However, my Dad was usually one of the early adopters with respect to changes. I think that he got his first tractor in about 1939. I would have been two years old so can't remember that far back. But I am sure that his first tractor was a little B John Deere. I heard him and my brothers talk about the time that my uncle Bill (Mom's little brother) backed up to the little John Deer, put his shoulders against one of the back wheels and lifted it off of the ground. He would have been pretty strong to do that. But Dad kept his horses and continued using them along with the little tractor for a few years. After one of his favorite team horses died, he didn't replace her and relied solely on tractors.

Dad's second tractor was a Z Minneapolis—Moline. I think it came with steel wheels but Dad soon put the rubber tires on it. His third tractor was an Oliver 70, and we really liked it. That was one of the reasons that he bought an Oliver implement store there in Arnold in 1947. Also, in 1947, just before he bought the implement store, he found a U Minneapolis—Moline for sale in Missouri. New tractors were hard to find the first few years after World War II ended because the factories had been busy producing war machinery. Not having a good farm truck at the time, Dad decided to drive the tractor home from Missouri. That proved to be quite a feat in itself. The U Minneapolis had a pretty fast road gear (at least fifteen miles per hour), but it still took several days to arrive at home. He said it was raining when he got to Lincoln Nebraska and he had to stop and buy a raincoat. Dad said the trip reminded him of his younger days when he and his family would drive cattle from their home in Kansas to the Sandhills of Nebraska. But that is another story.

The U Minneapolis burned LP gas (Liquid Petroleum). Dad liked the LP gas and later had all his tractors converted over to burn it. He would have the cylinder heads planed off to build up compression which got the most energy from the LP gas. Of course most of our later tractors were Olivers since Dad owned an Oliver store. One time my brother Dean and I were cultivating corn with a couple of Olivers, each taking two rows at a time (now days they take about eighteen rows at a time). Our tractors were running side by side. It was in the middle of a hot afternoon and we had probably been out too late the night before. I looked over at Dean and he was asleep (or nearly asleep) at the wheel but still keeping the tractor on the row. I shouted "Hey" as loud as I could. He woke up and cranked the steering wheel one way and plowed off some corn. Then he cranked it too far the other way and plowed off some more corn before he could get it back on the row again. Dad later saw the blank spots in the field and wondered what had happened. Dean and I have laughed about that many times since. He said I should have left him to sleep in peace instead of shouting at him. He was a little mad at me at first but soon got over it.

One more tractor story while we are on the subject (only one I promise). But I want to tell you about my latest tractor, the 1952 Oliver

77 that Jim will inherit while Bill gets the 1967 Ford wagon and Marla gets the Grandfather clock. I found this Oliver through an ad in the Omaha paper. It came from Iowa and was in pretty bad shape when I purchased it. But I have had barrels of fun restoring it to its present condition (and spent barrels of money on it too). Since that is the model of tractor I first learned to drive it is kind of special for me and brings back a lot of boyhood memories. In retirement, I enjoy driving it in parades (while Ma follows me in the Ford wagon), and entering it in tractors pulls. So far, the John Deeres have been out pulling it but it is so much fun trying to beat them. That is enough about tractors, now for a few car stories.

Cars

Dad had some Ford Model T's and Model A's that he used to talk about. I suppose they were the late twenties or early thirties models. He said sometimes they would have to back these models up a steep sandhill because they had more power in reverse than in low gear. Also the gravity feed fuel system worked better in reverse going up a steep hill. The first car that I can remember was Dad's 1937 Plymouth. I think he had it for about ten years. In the later years, he cut the back end off of it making it into a pickup (I did the same thing to an old hearse that your granddad Quig gave me but that is another story). It was the 37 Plymouth that I learned to drive on. Usually farm youths learned to drive at a young age. I was about twelve or thirteen years old when I learned to drive that old Plymouth pickup. I remember that we were out in a harvested wheat field and I was turning the car around in circles. But on one of the circles, I got too close to the grain truck and ran into its side. It punctured the radiator and Dad was not at all happy about it. He didn't spank me but had a serious talk with me about it.

The next vehicle that I can remember was Dads 1941 ford pickup. It had a flat head V/8 engine and would get about twenty miles to a gallon of gasoline. It was the pickup my brothers and I would ride in the back of to hold onto the cream cans going over the rough bridge. One time we went to Denver Colorado in it to take my uncle to his departure for World War II. On the way to Denver while my brothers and I were riding in the back end, I lost my hat. We pounded on the cab so Dad would stop for me to run back for my hat. In later years, I gave Dad a model of that black 41 Ford pickup for a gift. Mom gave it back to me after Dad passed on and it is on our basement bookcase now.

When I was in high school, I drove a 1947 Chevy pickup. It was in that pickup that your Mother and I would go on some of our first dates. It did have a pretty good heater in it for winter time use. Later we used the pickup around the farm to haul silage to the cows so it had a unique aroma smell for some of our dates. After I had dated your Mother for a while, she loaned me one half of the money needed to buy a 1952 Studebaker hardtop convertible—that was a nice car. I guess I never did get her paid back for the nice loan but we got married instead.

In 1958 your Mother and I had a good wheat crop so we bought a new Renault. It was a little four-door with a rear engine. The rear engine had to soon to be overhauled because of the dirty conditions of the country roads. I traded it for a 1957 Dodge pickup and then traded the pickup for a 1956 Packard. I had converted both the Dodge and the Packard to burn LP gas. Our next vehicles were a 1959 Studebaker Lark station wagon and a 1954 Ford pickup. After we had those for some time, Maryalice's dad (your Granddad Quig) gave us a 1960 Ford wagon to drive to Lincoln for college. Next we got a 1967 blue Ford station wagon. About that time Jim was getting old enough to drive so we got a 1964 Renault for him to learn on. It had a manual transmission but the clutch was a little grabbing which led to some pretty jerky starts for Jim. The gear shifting lever broke off and I installed a shovel handle for a gear shift (remember Jim)? Later Jim bought a 1964 red Chevy to drive to school. He overhauled the engine as a shop project in school. The police seemed to like to follow that red Chevy home once in a while—I guess it just attracted them for some reason.

When Marla was ready to start driving, we had a 1960 Ford Falcon for her to learn on. It was blue and white and I think part of the interior had been spray painted red (right Marla?) It also had a manual transmission or stick shift as sometimes called. One time during one of her driving lessons, we were driving by a cemetery. Marla said "How am I doing Dad" and I said fine. But then she began to get close to the side of the road and instead of pulling back onto the road, she cranked the steering wheel the other way and we went bouncing down in the ditch for a while. Later she had an orange Datsun followed by a 1970 Ford Maverick (one of which she bounced over some railroad tracks if my memory serves me right). I went with her and taught her how to bargain with the car dealer when she bought the Maverick.

We still had the 60 Ford Falcon for Bill to learn to drive with. I think we had a wild ride or two with driving lesson also. Later, we got Bill a 1970 black and red Ford Maverick to drive to school. I think it gave in to some wild rides too. There was a bent-over street sign down on Military Road that I had commented on. I found out later that it was bent because it was probably the only thing that kept the Maverick from upsetting as it went around that particular corner.

Bringing this chapter to an end, we had a 1981 Dodge Aries, a 1985 Chrysler Labaron and at present a 2003 Chevy Impala. This covers them all except the 1967 Ford station wagon that was given to us after your Granddad Quig passed on. We have restored it. We display it at the Nebraska State fair and drive it in parades (if I can talk your Mom into following me on the Oliver). I call it your Mom's car but she doesn't necessarily agree. I hope this chapter hasn't been too boring for you but it is hard to separate our lives from our cars—that is just the way it is. Now for some stories about hired men, outhouses and dirty tricks.

Hired Men, Outhouses, and Dirty Tricks

My Father had a rather large farming operation plus the Oliver implement store which I helped run at times. There was more work than he and his family could do so we usually had some hired help that stayed with us on the farm. Some of the hired men (usually young high school boys) could be quite mischievous at times. The first dirty trick that I want to tell you about involves the only toilet that farms had for many years, the old outhouse. The old outhouse did not have a hinged toilet seat around the two holes. That piece of engineering came later. It appears that the design of toilet seats may be coming full circle. When Maryalice and I were traveling last winter, we went into some newly designed restrooms that had no hinged toilet seats—just a solid rim like the outhouses had. If that is the case, it will put an end to the trivia complaining about who left the toilet seat up. At any rate, there is a lot of stories to be told about the old outhouses. For some of the young readers that may not know, the outhouse was a small house sitting over a pit that had been dug to hold the waste. Sometimes the outhouses would get pushed over on Halloween nights. There was a story about an outhouse that had been pushed over on to its door with a lady inside of it. The story goes that she had to crawl out through one of the holes. The old outhouse on the farm north of Arnold was located at the end of a well-traveled path with bushes growing on both sides. My brothers and sometimes a hired man thought it was quit humorous to jump out of the bushes at night and scare me on my way to the outhouse.

The outhouse was also a place you could go to just a get a nice little rest when the farm work got to be hard. We often accused each other of using that for an excuse to get out of some work. Maybe that is the reason they are still called "rest" rooms today. If someone on the farm asks, "where is the hired man," the logical answer might be "he is down at the 'rest' room." This next story involves one of those times but I was the one in the "resting" room. It was the ultimate of dirty tricks. It was in the first part of July and the hired man had bought some of the big "Cherry Bomb" firecrackers. He tied one onto the end of a long stick, lit it and shoved it down a crack along the outside of the outhouse. He shoved deep into the dodo. I was inside "resting" and not aware of what was going on outside. I heard this scrapping noise below me and leaned over to look down the other hole to see what it was. About that time the firecracker exploded and blew dodo all over the place. I had it on my bottom (which also smarted a little), some on my face, and worst of all on the brim of my new straw hat. Needless to say I was upset. About that time the outhouse door swung open and in looks the hired man and my brothers to see my reaction. They began rolling on the ground with laughter while I was busy tearing pages off of the old Sears and Roebuck catalog and trying to wipe myself somewhat clean. It was too big of a job and I had to go into the house for a bath. I was angry about the ordeal (to say the least) and vowed to get even if there was a way. The hired man had done the same thing to his little brother and thought it was great fun. The younger ones in a family are often the subject of these kind (or lesser) pranks that the older minds can dream up. I guess that is a fact of life. But I was determined to get even. I got some Cherry Bombs and tried to do the same thing to the hired man but never could get him to sit still long enough for the bomb to go off. I tried it several times and he never knew when it was going to happen until he heard the scraping noise. Then he would run out of the outhouse with his pants still down and say "how dumb do you think I am"? I would say "I don't know but you must be pretty dumb because you are the one that messed up your own 'resting' time. He could no longer rest in peace because he never knew when my next attempt would be. I guess that was my revenge—knowing that I had eliminated the hired man's resting periods. I think you can understand why I never have forgotten.

The last story in this chapter also involves the use of some those Cherry Bomb firecrackers. I was getting to the age (especially after receiving the training from my brothers and the hired man) where I began to think of some dirty tricks of my own to try. It was in July during wheat harvesting time and all of the harvest crew were sitting around the table eating dinner. I slipped away from the table, went outside and lit a Cherry Bomb near the dining room window. The Cherry Bombs made a real loud noise when they exploded. One of the harvest crew men had a spoon full of gravy in his hand when the bomb went off. He flipped the gravy ladle so hard that it threw gravy clear to the ceiling. Mom had to wipe the gravy off of the ceiling and she was not happy. This was not as dirty of a trick that had been played on me but it was rather cruel because the man that flipped the gravy was a war veteran and he was quite shaken by the explosion. That is about enough for this session. If any of these kind of things were tried now days, there would probably be all kinds of law suits resulting from them. I guess there are other things for entertainment like computer games and etc. to keep us out of trouble. Now to move on to storm stories.

Storms

Storms in Nebraska can be rather severe at times as most of you know. Following are a few that comes to my mind as I think back over time.

When I was about four or five years old, our house was struck by lightning. It was just before a hard rain storm. My brothers were setting in the yard inside of Dad's 1941 Ford pickup. When the lightning struck, there was a hen standing buy a steel walking plow in the yard. My brothers said the hen jumped about three feet in the air at the time. They thought that was rather humorous. Mom and I were standing inside of the house looking out of the kitchen screen door. When the bolt hit the house, I remember seeing a large ball of fire come across the metal screen door along with a large noise, crack. It did not burn or otherwise hurt Mom or me but it split two rows of shingles from the top to the bottom of the roof. Dad had to have the wooden shingles replaced on the roof. It could have been that same storm when lightning struck a wagon that a neighbor and his son were setting under. It burned them quite severe and they were in the hospital for a long length of time afterwards. That is about the closest to being struck by lightning when I was younger. However, our motorhome got struck with your Mother and I in it, when we were traveling in Florida after we were retired. It was raining very hard. We were parked at a military base. We heard the loud crack. Did not see any balls of fire but it blew out several light bulbs on the motorhome. That is enough about lightning. Just remember to respect it whether you are golfing, working outside, or whatever.

I guess now I will tell you about my experiences with tornados. If you live in the Midwest and especially Nebraska, you may have an encounter with a tornado at some period in time. When I was about four years old, our farm north of Arnold also nearly got hit with a tornado. Again, Mom and I were in the house and my brothers and Dad were out in the barn. About all that I remember was the windmill on the hill east of the barn was taken away. It also tore out some of our fence lines and killed a horse. I believe the horse got tangled up in some of the barbed wire fence and died. I guess that is about the closest I have been to tornados. I have seen several funnel clouds during violent storms.

Sometimes they will drop down to earth and other times they will go back up into the sky and dissipate among other mean looking clouds. If you watch the skies of Nebraska, you will see them sooner or later. Some of you might remember the tornado that hit Omaha in the mid to late seventies. Our National Guard unit was detailed up there to assist in security and clean up. I believe I was up there for about one week helping with that one.

Snow blizzards are the last kind of storm that I will be telling you about. When I was twelve years old, we had a bad one. It was called the blizzard of 1949. When a blizzard like that one hit the farms, all kind of things happened. The younger ones usually thought they were kind of fun but they were certainly to be respected too. Some of the fun things were, getting out of school, learning new games, and playing different kinds of games while being snowed in. Of course, the older ones that were responsible for our well-being and that of the livestock didn't think they were any fun at all. Some of the things that I remember about the blizzard of 1949 was that several hogs died because the storm drove them away from their hog houses and they froze to death. These same kind of storms have been known to drive whole herds of cattle into a sandhill lake where they all perish. In 1949, our country school teacher was snowed in with us for several days because her car had got stuck in the snow and Dad had brought her on the tractor. We learned how to play the card game cribbage during that storm. I still enjoy playing it with your Mother but she usually wins the game. We were snowed in for weeks at a time in 1949. Sometimes we would run rather low on food and have to improvise. I remember going to the grain bin and getting some wheat which we ground into flour by putting a tin plate in our meat grinder. Mom made some really good tasting muffins from that whole wheat flour. One other time when we were running low on supplies, the hired man living with us provided us with some good humor. He had remembered that Mom had canned several jars of wild plums and stored them in the storm cellar. The only problem was that there was at least a six- or seven-foot snow drift on top of the cellar door. Storm cellar doors were hinged nearly horizontal to ground level so all of the snow had to be scooped off to get the door open. The hired man scooped snow for several hours to get to the jars of wild plums. The problem was that he ate too many of them after he finally got to them. As I said before they can be pretty powerful and he found himself getting up in the middle of the night to make his way through the snow drifts to the old out house. It was kind of funny.

I am sure all of you that live in Nebraska can relate to some snow storms but they do not seem to be as severe as they were in the past. Maybe this global warming is changing our weather. A snow storm that I know Marla's family can remember is the one that came in October in the late 90's. We wanted to get one last fall camping trip in but winter came early that year and nailed us. We had the motorhome and the pull camper all parked at the Mahony State Park between Omaha and Lincoln. It started snowing in the middle of the night and dumped about two foot (Ok at least one foot) of heavy, wet, snow on us. I believe Marla and Terry had been to Lincoln and got back to the campers before it got too deep. Anyway, the next morning I was going to scoop a path between the campers. I was getting close to the little pull camper and was bent over scooping when Marla came out of the camper. The wind caught the door and blew it hard, hitting me square on top of the head. I did see a star or two and it reminded me a little like the time I got my head caught with the barn door. I don't think it knocked much sense into me (or out of me) but the cut was deep enough that they had to take me to the hospital to get stitches. The interstate was so clogged with traffic from the snow storm that it took about four hours to get to the hospital. We stayed at Marla's house in Waverly that night and went out the next day to get the campers. Trees and powerlines were down all over and required massive cleanup. I think that was the last fall camp-out we ever planned with Marla's family. It was certainly one to be remembered. Good old Nebraska weather. Now let us move on to some stories about fires.

Fires

It has been said that there are two sayings that really get farmers excited, especially my Dad. One of the sayings is "The cows are out" and the other one is of course "Fire." When I was about five years old, my Mom was using some gasoline (a no no) to start a fire in her wood/coal burning cook stove. I do not know exactly what happened but the fire got out of control and started burning the kitchen. Mom took a heavy blanket and threw it over the stove and wood pile and smothered out the blaze. She did get some minor burns. I was always amazed at her bravery to get the fire put out. Dad was working in a field about one mile from the house when a neighbor told him that he saw smoke coming from the kitchen and that the house was on fire. Dad jumped into his 1937 Plymouth, held the foot feed to the floor board and got home just as Mom was getting control of the fire. The rural fire truck got there right after Dad did. The fire had blackened all of the kitchen but did not spread to the other parts of the house. Our neighbors brought over some blankets and food for us to have. I remember thinking how nice it was of them to do that but that was (and still is) typical for people to help out in times of need. Dad had a carpenter repair the kitchen but he told Mom not to use gasoline to start anymore fires.

Prairie fires were very common in the area that we lived in. The occurrence of prairie fire is one theory of why much of the Great Plains area is treeless. Many times, they were started by a lightning strike. Sometimes, we would get let out of school to go help fight a prairie fire. It was not uncommon to drive several miles towards the smoke before arriving at the fire. If the wind changed directions, it could be a dangerous situation. Farmers and ranchers would use wet feed sacks and shovels to try to smother out the fireline. They would beat the fire line with a wet sack or throw shovels of dirt on it. It was a hot and dangerous job and of course no one wanted to see their pasture grass go up in smoke.

When I was in my teens, the implement store that I helped my Dad operate, was on fire at least three times. The first time was after a gas welder had exploded. The mechanics did not completely shut the acetylene gas off when they left for lunch. When they returned from lunch, something ignited the gas that had leaked out and there was a big explosion. The back-shop doors were large hanging doors that rolled on a rail. The explosion blew both doors straight out and the mechanics ran out under them, escaping any injury from the explosion and fire. They were lucky. The fire truck came but the fire did considerable damage before they got it under control.

One of the other implement store fires was not very serious but it did provide a good laugh for my brother Dean. I had been doing some arc welding at the shop bench and some sparks had fallen behind the bench. Later we heard a roaring sound and began to investigate. We discovered a fire in the wall behind the shop bench. It was nearly through the wall and was beginning to move up the outside of the building. Of course, we all got excited. I hollered "call the fire department" and ran outside to the hydrant. I do not remember turning the water on, but I had. I grabbed the garden hose and ran around to the south side of the shop where the fire was burning. The problem was when I got there, there was no water running from the hose. I began hollering to Dean to "turn the water on—turn the water on" but still no water came. I then threw down the hose and ran back around to the hydrant to see why he had not turned the water on. What I found was Dean doubled over in laughter. The hose had been ripped off of the faucet and water was just shooting onto the ground. I had run about three feet farther than the hose's length. I never felt anything and was just hollering at Dean for not turning the water on. Like I said, fire has a way of getting people excited. The fire truck came and extinguished the fire before much damage was done but Dean had a good laugh and we still chuckle about it even to this day.

Pets

As you know, pets are a very important part of our lives. They make interesting and playful companions for the young and old alike. In addition to their companionship, we enjoy teaching them to do tricks and obey commands. Although much could be written, following are just a few of my memories about pets. Cats are a favorite pet for many. Some of my first memories about cats were when our farm mother cats would have a new batch of kittens. Us kids liked to find the new kittens and play with them. Every few days, the mother cat would move her kittens to a new hiding place and we would begin the hunt all over. She would pick each kitten up very gently in her mouth and carry it to the new hiding place. I always thought that was kind of interesting. She could have been hiding them from us or she could have been hiding them from the tomcats. Tomcats sometimes killed the newborn kittens because the kittens were possibly seen as territorial threats—I had a hard time understanding that as a child. When the kittens got older and while we were milking cows, we enjoyed squirting streams of milk at them and watching them catch some of the milk in their mouths.

It has been said that cats have nine lives. The cat we have now (Abbie) and are enjoying in our older age has proven that statement to be somewhat true. She was given to us by Bill and Kim. She had used one of her nine lives on a military base in Texas. The base housing air—condition had quit working and when Bill came home, Abbie was nearly dead from the heat. He had to put her in a cool shower to bring her back to life. And then Jim saved her life once here in Lincoln. I had pushed the button to close the big garage door without a thought about Abbie. Jim just happens to be walking out to the garage when he saw that Abbie was being squashed under the door. He came running back to the house and pushed the button to raise the door off of Abbie. We took her to the Vet who said it was a close call. Another time she got out of our car at Grand Island on our way home from Arnold. We got to Lincoln before we noticed her absence. Bill and I drove back to Grand Island and found her under parked cars at the restaurant where we had stopped to eat three hours earlier. Since then on our winter trips to Texas, she ran away and we thought she was gone for good, but somehow, she has always been reunited with us. I won't go into all of those details except to say again she has used up most of her nine lives.

Of course, dogs are another favorite pet. The first dog that I can remember was a shepherd we called Pal. I had picked him from a liter at the neighbor's farm and he was a special pet for me. He was a good cattle dog. He helped me drive a herd of cows from our farm five miles north of Arnold to the farm thirteen miles west of Arnold. It took us most of a day and I could not have done it without the help of Pal. When the cows would get into a grove of trees, he would chase them back on to the road again. On the farm west of Arnold, I also taught Pal to go bring the cows in from the pasture even if they were over the hill and out of sight. Another special dog for me in my younger days was a little dog named Dicky. He was a little rat terrier. During the summer months, I had built me a room from straw bales and was sleeping in the barn haymow. I taught Dickey dog to climb the ladder to the haymow. We thought that was a neat trick. Another special pet for all of us after you kids were born was Snoopy dog. He was a little white spotted dog about the same size as Dickey dog. You kids taught him some tricks and he would go on camping trips with us. He got his side ripped open by a big dog while we were living in Lexington—remember that Marla? That night after the Vet had stitched him up, he dragged himself to the upstairs bedroom to sleep by Jim. He was a special pet, especially for Jim I think. I think this is enough about pets. I don't want to bore you too much. You all have had pets of your own and you know how special they can be. Some that come to my mind right now are Duke, Simon, Butch, Ricky, Calvin, Hobbs, Otis, Milo, Gus, Sparky, and Mattie. Even though we (especially Mom and I) sometimes treat them as equals, God did not intend for animals to be equal to humans. God said to man "have dominion over every living thing that moveth upon the earth" (Genesis Chap. 1, vs 28) He gives us pets to care for and be with for a while and then they go on to pet heaven, leaving us with some very special memories. Yes, pets are a very important part of our lives. Now I want to move on to some stories about the way we interpret or misinterpret words.

Play on Words

Like I said before, I have always had a way of taking things very literally or the wrong way. This has hindered the communication process over the years but also provided some humor. The first one that comes to mind is when I was in my late teens and working in my Fathers farm implement store. Some of my fondest memories come from those years in the implement store. But on this occasion, my brothers and my dad were talking about what had caused one of the shop fires. My dad said this one particular fire had been caused by a parts washer (meaning a tank of fluid with a pump to wash off greasy motor parts). My mind heard the word "parts washer" and locked in on it. I said, "Did you say the fire was started by a parts washer?" They said "yes." I said "parts washer"? They said "yes, parts washer." I thought a little while (but not long enough). With a blank look on my face, I made a circle by touching my forefinger to my thumb, held it up and said, "How could a little parts washer start a fire?" Of course, they all started laughing. I don't blame them—it was rather humorous. They finally clarified what kind of parts washer it was but teased me about it for some time after. As I think back on it, I am glad I was able to provide them with some much-needed humor.

The next story I will share also happened at the implement store that I was operating for Dad. It was a few years later, after your Mother and I were first married. It was in the spring of the year during corn planting time. These were busy times and I would usually go to the farm to help get the corn planted. This was part of the flexibility required for family operations such as ours. But it required your mother (bless her heart) to operate the implement store while I was helping on the farms. I don't know if you remember, Jim, but Mom would take you along to play in the show room until your Granddad Quig would come to get you. Your Mom would sell parts and seed corn to the farmers as needed. I tried to check back with her occasionally to see how thing were going. Anyway, like I said, it was a busy time of the year. Brother Dean and I had stopped at the implement store to pick up some seed corn that was to be delivered. Some of our newly planted corn had been washed out and would have to be replanted. We were nervous (at least I was). It was getting late in the year for replanting and here we were (burning daylight as Dean would say) waiting for our replant corn to be delivered. We had called the seed company earlier and it was nearly an hour past the time it was to be delivered. About that time a pickup truck arrived. It had a decal on its door signifying the brand of seed corn we were waiting for. I told Dean, "Here's the corn, finally." The driver approached us and said, "Do you want a sign?" I thought he said, "Do you want to sign?" I said, "Where is the corn?" He looked puzzled and said again, "Do you want a sign?" My mind was locked in on replanting corn and I said urgently "I am not signing anything until I see the corn, where is the corn?" By this time, Dean had it figured out that the driver was delivering advertising signs, not seed corn. Dean was laughing and trying to explain to me what the deal was. I think our seed corn came not too long after that but Dean and I still laugh about it even today when we get together.

The last story I will share on this subject occurred after Jim was married and raising a family. He had been working on the brakes of one of his vehicles. Some of the parts were frozen and he was unable to get them apart. It was in the winter time and I had purchased some of a product called Heet to prevent gas line freezing. He called me, explained the problem and asked for some advice. He said, "Do you think it would do any good to put heat on it"? I said "Heet"? Yes, heat. "I said "Heet" Why don't you use WD40? Jim explained he meant flame heat not liquid Heet but it was another one of those times when we had a good laugh. Now let us move on to the final but more serious chapter about Life-Changing Events.

Life-Changing Events

This will be the last chapter on Memories, so the end is in sight. Then, I will type up what your mother has written, and we will get them added to your books. I don't know quite where to start so guess I will just ramble on for a while and then quit. Thanks Bill for keeping us going on this until we got the job done—it has been kind of a neat experience.

The first life-changing event I will share is about the most important day of my life—the day that I met that wonderful Mother of yours. God was good to me that day. It was at the beginning of my sophomore year in high school. I went to Stapleton for my freshman year and to Arnold for the second year. I saw her in the halls, maybe it was the first day of school. She said I flirted a little bit with her. I remember she used to wear a red and green checkered dress that I liked. My first close meeting of her was at a dance soon after that first day of school. Brother Dean was good about taking his little brother to dances and dates—he was a nice brother. He took me along to a dance and I saw this pretty girl again that kind of made my heart flutter a little. I asked her to dance and she did. We two—stepped our way through it and before the evening was over, I ask if I could take her home after the dance. Dean had asked to take her friend home so it was kind of a double date. I can't say that it was love at first sight but there was something about this nice pretty girl that just attracted me to her. On the way home, Dean took the long way home through the Arnold park and we sat and smooched for a while. So that was our first date. We continued dating steady through high school and beyond. Of course, we had our share of fights but there never was another girl that I wanted to go with after we met. We got married the first year after high school on December 2, 1956. Next year will be our fiftieth wedding anniversary. Fifty wonderful years. We have had our share of fights over the years but the first five years were the most fights. After that they have been less and less. Hang in there Brenda and Jim. Your mom is the most considerate person. She always gives me the largest half of anything she divides for sharing. After we were first married, we lived with my folks for a short period of time until Dad got a house fixed up to live in. We moved into that first house before the inside bathroom was finished so your mom got to experience the "old outhouse" for a while. It was just an old farmhouse two miles east of my folk's place. With no insulation, the farm houses were cold and drafty in the winter time. Your Mom adjusted well even though she had always been a city girl.

God blessed us with our first born, Jim, on April 6, Easter Sunday, 1958 (see poem written previously). It was during a late snow blizzard at the Callaway hospital. What a special day that was. We tried to be good parents even though we made our share of mistakes in parenting. One time we thought Jim had drank some gasoline so we drove him to the doctor in North Platte but they said he was OK. And he hasn't run out of gas since then because he still works hard at everything he does. Someday you will want to slow down and retire Jim—it is great. Jim earned his Eagle Scout rank and has made us very proud. All of our children have been very special and made us equally proud.

God blessed us again on October 7; 1961. That was when our only, very special, daughter was given to us (also see poem written previously). Marla was born in a North Platte hospital after a couple of previous false alarms. One false alarm, we stayed with some friends at North Platte all night but nothing happened. It was a forty—five-mile trip to the hospital one way. Marla has also made us very proud. She excelled in synchronized swimming. She earned the rank of Job's Daughter Queen with her mom working in the organization to help her through the different levels.

About a year and a half after Marla was born, your Mother had a miscarriage. I will never forget that night. Your Mom started bleeding bad and actually had it at home. We put it in a towel and started the forty—five- mile trip to the hospital. She was still bleeding hard and I had the foot feed held to the floor to get there as quick as possible. That 1952 Studebaker that your Mom helped me buy saw 100 miles an hour that night. When we arrived at the hospital, I ran around the car, grabbed your Mom up in my arms and ran to the emergency door of the hospital (I don't remember her being heavy to carry at all). It was locked (I think it was about 1:00 a.m. in the morning). I hollered real loud and banged on the door. A nurse soon came and they got a wheel chair to put her in and took her to an emergency room. They gave her a blood transfusion and kept her in the hospital for a few days. The doctor never told us if the baby was a boy or a girl. He said it was probably good that it happened because it had been a troublesome pregnancy and many time those babies are not normal.

After we left the farm and moved to Lincoln to go to college, God blessed us yet again. Our very special youngest son, Bill, was born on September 5, 1966 (Labor Day). He too has been a real blessing and has made us proud parents once again. I didn't get a poem written about him but he wrote a very special story about the time I was in the hospital with cancer surgery in 1985. Thanks Bill, that meant a lot to me. He earned his Eagle Scout rank and is making a career as a naval aviator in the U.S. Navy.

Way to go kids! You have all made us proud parents and now you all have spouses and kids of your own to make us prouder. Each one is a very special gift from God and I will leave you to write about your life memories someday. I won't leave, however, without mentioning the names of each of these very special gifts of God. They are Brenda, Terry, Kim, Veronica, Bob, Alisha, Christy, Niki, Ronnie, Micah, Kyra, Tessa, Tyler, and Jacey. We will always welcome more Grandkids if you feel so inclined but God might be about done with those kinds of blessings for now. We just thank *HIM* for each one of you and we love you all.

Before we leave this subject of life-changing events, I want to share some of the things that I have learned about stages in life and finish up with some things about my spiritual growth.

I told one of the grandkids, Micah I believe, that life is a series of adjustments (at least three major ones). The first major adjustment as I see it is adolescence—the period of going from a child to an adult. And like all stages in life, it is more traumatic for some than others. Your body is going through changes, your hormones may be running wild, and it can be a tough time to get through. You want to get established into adulthood but yet you do not want to leave your childhood either. It is a stage we all get through one way or the other. Bill gave me a cute Father's Day card this year. It said "Dad when I was a child, you knew everything about everything. When I became a teenager, you didn't know anything at all. Now you know everything again. It must have been a stage you were going through— right"?

The next major adjustment period is the mid—life one. Again, this can be very traumatic for some while some do not even feel much difference. Your mother did not feel much difference while I had more of a traumatic one. I took a class at the University about it and read a good book called "Passages" by Gail Sheehy. The best definition that I have run across is "that period of time in your life when you really realize your own mortality. When you start counting the time you have left on this earth instead of the time you have been here." You may wake up some morning, look in the mirror and see some gray hair and think, "hey, someday I am going to die." People react differently to it. Some will have the desire to seek out a younger companion or look for other ways to change their life. It is a period that causes some divorces. Mine showed up as an overreaction to the fear of death that precipitated into some hypochondriac conditions. When I became the same age as my brother Bob was when he died of an aneurysm, it hit me. Also, a neighbor of that same age had just keeled over from a heart attack. I was convinced that I too was going to die soon. My mind started playing tricks on me. I would get chest pains and other symptoms of heart problems. My doctor was somewhat puzzled about it. He arranged for me to receive some counseling. That, along with self-education about the subject and the loving care and understanding from your wonderful Mother, all helped me get me through it. I only share this with you in hopes that it may be some help to some of you if yours is a traumatic one. Self-education about the subject is very helpful and can alleviate some of the trauma. Sometimes one does not realize what is happening to their body at the time but realizes it later. I think that is about all I have to say about the mid—life adjustment. Now for the old age one.

The third major adjustment period is that of adjusting to old age and to the subject of dying. I am not willing to admit that I am there yet. I may just stay in the middle life one forever. The old age one can be a traumatic one too. Sometimes, when one reaches the same age as your parents were when they died, it can hit you. Your Mom and I have seen both of our parents pass on now and we will ready when our time comes. We plan on being around at least another thirty years because we are both in good health now at sixty-eight years old. Of course, faith has and will help us all get through the adjustments of life. That is what I want to share with you now.

Our faith grows and will never quit growing as long as we live. There is always more to learn. Some may have a big growth period (the more fundamental churches call it being saved) while others experience more gradual growth periods. My salvation has been more gradual but with some identifiable periods of more growth at different times in my life. It does not matter just HOW it happened but that it did happen. God is in control. Jesus said, "The wind bloweth where it listeth, and thou heareth the sound thereof, but canst not tell whence it cometh, and whither it goeth: so is every one that is born of the spirit." John 3:8. He also said, "You shall know the truth and the truth will set you free"(John 8:32). "He touched and made me whole", as it says in the hymn. As I said before, God was good to me the day I met your Mother. Since I met her, I have slowly been transformed from a little heathen in the sandhills that got drunk on Saturday nights into the growing Christian that I am today. Jim has helped me along on this path too—thanks Jim. Like I said, we will never get there completely, we will never be perfect (God and Jesus are the only perfect ones) but with Gods help, we will never quit growing. About these believing things, you either believe that the Bible is true or that it is a bunch of Hooey—one of the two. I believe that it is true. Christ is truth. He said He would be killed and rise in three days, and it happened. He said he has gone to prepare a place for us to be with him, and he has. One cannot deny truth. Lee Stroble's books on faith that Jim recommended to me were a tremendous faith builder. Strobel was an atheist and a lawyer before he started looking for the truth. I would recommend his books to anyone who wants to confirm and grow in their faith. True believers don't need proof "Blessed are they who have not seen and yet have believed." We all have a little bit of doubting Thomas in us but it sure is nice to have your faith reinforced by books like Strobel's. When we die, I believe that Jesus will come and lead us just as he said he would. Many people, who have experienced near death, tell about a bright light that comes and leads them through a tunnel or something. Jesus is light. I saw a bright light in a very vivid dream soon after your Granddad Quig died. At that time, I thought maybe it was his spirit telling me to take good care of his little girl (your Mom) but with more thought, I think it was Jesus. He is light. That was one of my growth periods. After your Mom and I were married, she gently talked me into getting baptized. That was a beginning for me. It did not affect me too much at the time but was just the beginning of a faith building process. I was not raised in a Christian home so it was all new to me. My Dad kind of talked against God even though his Mother had exposed him to the Bible at a young age. I don't know why he didn't appear to believe but he and Mom had enough exposure that I do think they made it to Heaven along with both of Maryalice's parents. And we will see them in Heaven one day. All they had to do is believe and accept Jesus even at the last moment before death and He would take them to be with Him as He promised He would. He is truth. He is God's gift to us for our salvation and He was given by grace. We cannot earn it by good deeds. All we have to do is believe and accept Him and then we will want to do good deeds for Him.

I think I am about ready to sign off here. I hope you have enjoyed reading this as much as I have writing it for you. I want to get these books presented to you soon. Thank you all for reading this and hanging on to the end. God Bless you all and we will see you in Heaven one day.

Love, Dad August, 2005

Keith's Family
Top: Keith's Mom and Dad
Brothers Bob and Dean; and Sister Gloria
Bottom: Keith at around eight years old and high-school
graduation. Bottom Right: Keith's parents, Loyd, and Irene
Sheets.

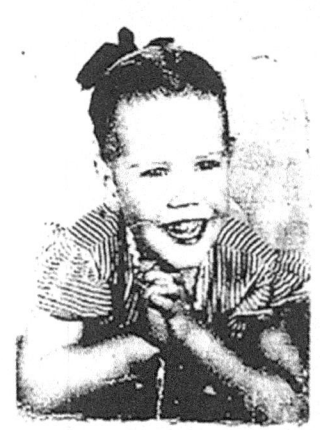

Maryalice's Family.
Top: Maryalice at four years

Bottom Right: Maryalice's Mom,
Dad, Maryalice, and Brother Charles

Bottom Center: Maryalice's high
school graduation.

Bottom Left: Maryalice's parents,
Charles, and Dorthy Quig

Top: Maryalice and Keith, engaged December 1955.
Bottom: Married, December 2, 1956

Top Left: Keith, Maryalice and Jim at the red farm house about 1960

Top Right: Maryalice, Marla and Pal dog at the red farm house about 1964.

Bottom Left: Jim, Marla, Bill in the Lincoln house in 1967

Bottom Right: Keith and Bill at Lincoln House in 1967

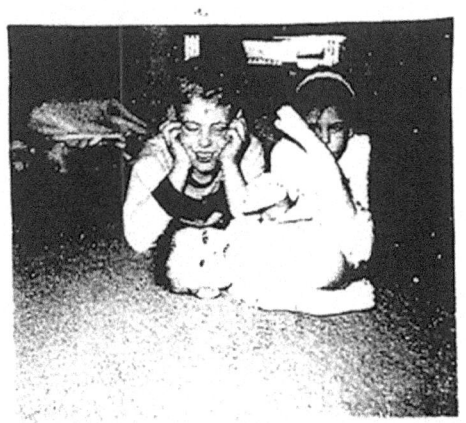

Top Left: Bill, Marla, Jim and Keith College graduation in 1969

Top Right: Maryalice gets her college degree in 1982 after helping Keith get his,

Bottom Left: Jim, Bill and Marla in their Sunday church going clothes.

Bottom Right: Family picture at Granddad and Gradma Quig's house in Arnold Nebraska, Easter.

Accomplishments that make parents proud.

Top Left: Jim earns his Eagle rank in Boy Scouts in 1970

Center: Bill earns his Eagle rank in 1980.

Bottom: Marla earns her Job's Daughters Honor Queen in 1979. Way to go kids.

Family Vacations.

Top Left: Bill (with fish) and Granddad Sheets on Rio Grande River place in NM

Top Right and Center: Keith, Marla and Bill, same river

Bottom Left: Marla, Jim, Bill and Maryalice in Colorado.

Bottom Right: The whole family at Florida's Disney World in April, 2002

High School Graduates.

Jim's in 1976.

Marla's in 1979.

Bill's in 1985.

Adventure Trips.

Top: Jim and Keith back packing in Colorado near Steamboat Springs.

Bottom: Bill and Keith white water rafting Vale, Colorado.

Starting Their Lives Together.

Top: Jim and Brenda, 2001.

Bottom Left: Marla and Terry, 1986

Bottom Right: Bill and Kim, 1992

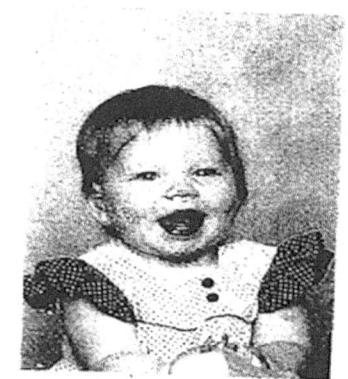

The Next Generation

Top: Jim and Wendy's children, Bob, Veronica and Alisha.

Middle: Marla and Terry's children, Micah, Tessa and Kyra.

Bottom: Bill and Kim's children, Tyler and Jacey.

Top: Family and Christmas in 1991.
Left to right: top row, Maryalice, Keith, Terry, Kyra, Marla, Micah, Mom Quig;
Front row: Bill, Kim, Bob, Wendy, Veronica, Jim
Bottom: Brenda and girls join the family. Christmas 2001.
Left to right, back row, Bob, Nicky, Christy, Brenda, Jim.
Front row, Alisha and Rony.

Alaska Cruise 2010, Jim's family,
Left to right: Alisha, Bob, Veronica, Jim, and Brenda Sheets

Alaska Cruise 2010, Marla's family
Left to right; Tessa, Kyra, Micah, Marla and Terry Kurtenbach

Alaska Cruise 2010, Bill's family
Left to right: Tyler, Jacey, Kim, and Bill Sheets
Bottom: Keith and Maryalice's 50th

Maryalice's Letter

Dear Kids,

I, Maryalice Quig, was born June 25, 1937, at 7:00 PM at home in Beaver City Nebraska to Dorothy Marie (Tompkins) Quig and Charles Durward Quig. I was named after my two grand mothers, Mary (Neal) Tompkins and Alice (Clute) Lyons. I had one brother, Charles. We were never close. There was three years difference in our age.

The first three years of my life were in Beaver City Nebraska where my parents operated a funeral home. I have no recollection of these first three years. When the funeral home wasn't profitable during the depression, we moved to Oxford Nebraska where both of my grandparents lived. My Folks helped my grandparents, George and Mary Tompkins, operate a restaurant for a couple of years. I have a few recollections of these two years at my grandparents, like my Granddad Tompkins' death and funeral.

We then moved to Gering Nebraska where my dad worked for Bros Brothers Furniture store and funeral home. Here is where I started school going through second grade. I remember our house there and we went back there about ten years ago and located the house. I remember walking catty corner to the park at the end of the block and walking a few blocks to the swimming pool (where I never learned to swim). During this period, I remember having scarlet fever and Dad being quarantined out of the house for three weeks. I also had chicken poxs and measles which caused me to miss my last day of school picnic. During the time I had scarlet fever, I listened to the radio a lot and it was at this time when we heard that President Roosevelt had died. This was during World War Two. I remember going grocery shopping and the ration coupons that we had to use. I also had my first experience with a commercial hot cocoa mix that came in a big bag which we kept in the basement. I used to go down to the basement and eat it dry by the spoonful. We mixed it with milk instead of hot water. During this time, I would have a lot of bad dreams about the Germans coming to get us and we would hide in the basement corners. Some of the war news came from the news reel at the movies. To go to the movies, we would take a quarter. The movie cost about five cents and popcorn was the same price.

One time when I went shopping with my mother, I left a fig Newton cookie on the porch where I was playing house. When I came back, I started to eat one of the cookies and I crunched into a razor blade that someone had slipped into the cookie—no damage done.

The summer after second grade we moved to Ainsworth Nebraska where my Dad worked for another funeral home. We lived for a short while upstairs over the funeral home then we moved into a house down the alley from the school. My biggest recollection of this town was one day I was playing on the equipment at the school when the sirens and the church bells started ringing. I was scared and ran home but it was a celebration for the end of the war.

In November of 1945 (that same year) my parents bought the funeral home at Arnold Nebraska. My mother played the church organ at every town we lived in and continued playing until she was around eighty-seven years old. Fifty of those years were at the Arnold church. She started playing in churches when she was twelve years old. She also organized the Job's Daughters Bethals in Gering and Arnold where I earned the rank of Honored Queen in 1955. Mom was a beautiful musician and her talents are greatly missed as are both of my parents. All of my school experiences, friends and other memories were in Arnold. Having friends stay overnight was somewhat of a scary experience for them since we lived in the funeral home. Life living in the funeral home was all I knew so the experience was normal to me. My toys and playing were limited to my bedroom and closet. I had my dolls and kitchen set up in my tiny closet which was adjacent to the morgue. My friends and I would take our dolls and buggy down town and walk the streets. Due to poor health, my grandmother Tompkins moved to Arnold to live by us. We shared a bedroom until her house was built behind our house.

During my teenage years, I worked at the theater through high school. The farmers would come to town on Wednesday and Saturday nights for shopping. The town was buzzing. There would be a show every night, but Wednesdays and Saturdays were always crowded. We walked everywhere so we walked to town and home again and would spend many hours walking around and around the main business district; of course flirting with the boys and hoping to get a ride home or an escort. High school was a happy time for me with football, basketball, pep club and all of the musical events. I loved music, sang in the glee club, was in sextet and played the clarinet in the band. I became first clarinet player by my junior year. I also was a cheer leader in the seventh, eighth and twelfth grades. We had roller skating in Arnold periodically and dances at least once a month. I loved those dances.

During the summer of my junior year, I started working at the Community Hospital. At this time I was considering becoming a nurse. I started working at the Hospital again after high school and continued working there until I became pregnant with Jim. I applied for nursing school but since I was going with Keith and the hospital was something I loved and was already working there, I decided not to go.

I met Keith my sophomore year in school. He went to Arnold that one year of high school. We dated some as sophomores. He was so good looking and a good flirt. For his junior and senior year, he went to Gandy but we continued dating. He had my heart from the beginning. By the end of our junior year we were "going steady" and you know the rest of the story. My social life consisted of movies, dances, roller skating, football, basketball, baseball and dating. Dates in our day was usually sitting with someone in the movies or an escort home. Very seldom were we taken to a movie or dance. Once Keith and I were a steady couple, we did go to the movies together.

I don't have unusual stories as my life was very normal. Methodist Youth Fellowship (MYF) was an important part of my life. All my friends were involved. I accepted Jesus as my Lord and Savior at the age of sixteen. This greatly influenced my moral standards. I didn't drink nor smoke nor did I have a desire to. I had a very happy childhood and teenage years. I was not a rebellious child. My life was full with good friends, good parents and a good social life.

During this time, life was much simpler and fairly safe. We were raised in good times after the war. Although my folks were struggling financially, I never realized it. I always worked so I bought a lot of my own clothes. My wages at the hospital were 75 cents an hour. My wages at the theater were around $5 or $6 per week. A one day stay at the hospital cost $8.00.

Keith (Dad) went to the Army in December, 1955, after we were graduated. That Christmas, we became engaged and were married the following December. After marriage we lived on the farm for ten years. Milking cows was a chore I learned to do on the farm but I wished I had not learned and I never missed it when we left. Farming was hard work, late hours but also a rewarding life. It had its pros and cons. Jim was born in 1958 and Marla came along in 1961. When Jim and Dad came to the hospital to pick us up, Jim (three) ask if she would wet her pants.

In 1966, we decided to leave the farm so dad could go to college and start a new life. At this time we discovered that Bill would soon join the family. During those college days, money was tight. We looked for cheap or free entertainment. We had some of the best years of our life. After college, we moved to Lexington for six months and O'Neal for nine months with dad's job. Then Dad found a job in Lincoln with the Natural Resource Commision. We moved back to Lincoln and to old friends where you kids grew up. I worked as para educator for eight years before I went to college to become a teacher, graduating in 1982. I spent sixteen years as a teacher before we retired in 1999.

Love, Mom August, 2005

My Grandparents

My Dad's (Charles Durward Quig) parents were Charles Avery Quig and Alice Clute. Charles Avery died of blood poisoning when my dad was sixteen years old so I didn't know him. Alice Clute then married Charles Lyons my step granddad. He is the only granddad that I remember. He was a mortician and that is how my dad got interested in the profession. Grandma was a partner in the business. She was a good knitter and we looked forward to a pair of knitted mittens each Christmas. They lived at Oxford Nebraska. Alice died on October of 1953 and Charlie died in December of 1954. Alice had four children (Loraine, Dad, Ray, and Ruth) and Charles had one daughter, Grace.

My mother's (Dorothy Marie Tompkins) parents were George Ellet Tompkins and Mary Neal. Granddad was a conductor on the railroad so they moved a lot. He died in March of 1940. He was an only child. My Grandmother and Granddad (before his death) operated a restaurant in Oxford Nebraska in their later years. Grandmother continued in the restaurant after his death until her health failed. She was sixteen when she was married. Mother was their only child. Grandma was one of five children being the second oldest. She had one sister, Stacia, and three brothers, Harry, John, and Frank. There were only two children descendants from this family. I think Mary's father, Clayton, was a teacher. Grandmother was a skilled seamstress and made many quilts as well as clothes for Mother, and myself. She also made some of Marla's clothes and even some for Jim. She lived with/by us from 1946 until her death in 1964.

Maryalice Quig Sheets August 2005

About the Author

The author, Keith Sheets, grew up on a farm near Arnold, Nebraska. He had 2 older brothers, Bob, Dean, and a younger sister, Gloria. He graduated from high school in Gandy Nebraska in 1955 and married MaryAlice Quig in 1956. To this union were born 3 children, Jim, Marla, and Bill. He graduated from the University of Nebraska in 1969 with a degree in Agricultural Economics. He then attended the Nebraska Law School for one year. He worked for the Nebraska Natural Resources Service as an economist for 11 years and ended his career employed for 27 years by the Federal Government Natural Resources Conservation Service